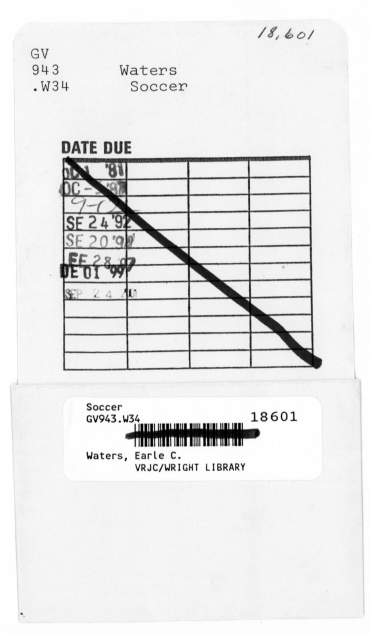

SOCCER

SOCCER

Earle C. Waters

Paul E. Hawk

John Y. Squires

ARCO PUBLISHING COMPANY, INC.

New York

PUBLISHED 1973 BY ARCO PUBLISHING COMPANY, INC.
219 PARK AVENUE SOUTH, NEW YORK, N.Y. 10003

COPYRIGHT © 1943, 1950, 1961 BY UNITED STATES NAVAL INSTITUTE,
ANNAPOLIS, MARYLAND

LIBRARY OF CONGRESS CATALOG CARD NUMBER 72-91945
ISBN 0-668-02463-1

PRINTED IN THE UNITED STATES OF AMERICA

Preface

THE FIRST EDITION of this book was prepared from material used by hundreds of coaches and instructors who trained aviation cadets under the U. S. Navy's V-Five Program during World War II. Since World War II, this book has found wide usage in programs outside the field of naval aviation training and has been up-dated as necessary to include new techniques and methods. Particular emphasis has been placed on adapting coaching experience and lesson planning to the proper graduations of high school and college instruction and competition.

T. J. HAMILTON
Rear Admiral, USN (Ret.)

Executive Director
Athletic Association of Western Universities
San Francisco, California

Introduction to Third Edition

Soccer, or association football, is a universal game. If the United States is to develop better players to represent us in the World Cup and Olympic Games, this sport must be promoted to a greater extent than it is now in schools, colleges, and amateur leagues. It is also necessary to raise to a higher level the caliber of the coaching of the beginning players.

In this edition the revision committee has added a new chapter on principles which could be helpful to anyone engaged in coaching. The book has been brought up to date to meet the new intercollegiate rules except for the change in the marking of the penalty area. All diagrams, save one, show the international penalty area marking. The exception, on page 83, shows the intercollegiate marking. Additional material has been added to the chapters on history, team play, drills, and games.

It is hoped that this book will contribute to the advancement of this sport by improving the knowledge and techniques of those who take the time to read and study it carefully.

E.C.W.
P.E.H.
J.Y.S.

Table of Contents

PAGE

PREFACE v

INTRODUCTION TO THIRD EDITION vii

CHAPTER

I   HISTORY OF SOCCER 3

II   FACILITIES, EQUIPMENT AND SAFETY SUGGESTIONS 7
    Facilities 7
    Equipment 10
    Safety Suggestions 13

III WARM-UP PERIODS 15

IV   INDIVIDUAL FUNDAMENTALS 18
    Long Kicks 19
    Short Kicks 29
    Passing 34
    Trapping 34
    Dribbling 39
    Heading 41
    Ball Control 42
    Tackling and Charging 44
    Charging 47
    Obstructing 48
    Throwing 49
    Running 50
    Feints and Pivots 50
    Fundamental Skills Evaluated 54

V   THE GOALKEEPER'S SKILLS 57

VI   ANALYSIS OF INDIVIDUAL POSITIONS 67
    Goalkeeper 68
    Fullbacks 70
    Halfbacks 71
    Center Halfback 72
    Suggestions for All Backs 73
    Wings (Outside Forwards) 75

CHAPTER PAGE

Inside Forwards 77
Center Forward 78
Suggestions for All Forwards 79

VII GAME SITUATIONS 81
Penalties 101
Suggestions for the Referee 109
Interpretations of Laws of Soccer (Questions—Answers) .. 110

VIII TEAM OFFENSE AND DEFENSE 118
Sane Soccer for Elementary Schools 126
Switch Plays 127

IX PRINCIPLES OF COACHING 129

GLOSSARY 136

APPENDIXES 139
I. Drills on Fundamentals 141
II. Games to Make Practice Fun 159
III. Intercollegiate Marking of Field, 1961 167

INDEX 169

SOCCER

CHAPTER I

History of Soccer

The origin of soccer is difficult to trace. The ancient Greeks had a game called "Harpaston," wherein a ball was propelled by any possible means over lines which were usually at opposite ends of a town and were defended by the opposing teams. Throwing was probably the most commonly used method of advancing the ball, as the meaning of the word "Harpaston" is to hurl forward. The Romans adopted this game under the name of "Harpastum" and made of it a military sport for the training of warriors. The Romans limited the advancement of the ball to kicking it with the foot or striking it with the hand. It became very popular with the Roman warriors and all were urged to play it. "The popularity of this type of game probably prompted Martial, the court poet of Domitian, as early as 40 A.D. to advise all men and boys to play it."[1]

When the Romans invaded England they took this game with them, and it may be that from this game our present sport had its origin. At least we do know that kicking games were in use throughout the ages; that soccer was not an invented game but one that went through a process of evolution. The name of football became attached to it either because it was a game played with the foot as a means of advancing the ball or because it was played on foot and not on horseback.

The early form of the game in England was mob football played by the common people. There were no limits as to how many players each side could use, and as the goals were often as far as a mile apart, the games usually lasted for hours. Games were played between one camp of soldiers and another, between the married men and the bachelors of a town, between parish and parish, and between trades. It became the feature attraction on all festival days and was looked forward to by the common people. Shrove Tuesday, or the Tuesday prior to the beginning of Lent, became the great soccer football day in England. On this day vast crowds would turn out to play or watch the game. With so many players on a side and no rules enforced, the game was rough and led to many fights and injuries. This, together with the fact that the game became more popular with the soldiers than archery, led the rulers of England to outlaw the sport. In 1314 Edward II, in 1349 Edward III, in 1389 Richard II, in 1401 Henry IV, in 1504 Henry VIII, and in 1581 Queen Elizabeth all forbade the game to be played. Queen Elizabeth only ruled against it's being played in London, no doubt prompted by the damage it caused to the stores when played in the streets. The clergy objected to soccer's being played on Sunday and therefore were opposed to the game. The Scottish kings James I and James III ruled against the game. As it was a game of the common people, the aristocrats were opposed to it.

Football, or Soccer, in the olden times, found no place in the annals of knight-errantry, but it found a warm corner in the breasts of common people.

[1] Coyer, Hubert E., *The Coaching of Soccer;* W. B. Saunders Co., 1937, p. 20.

Football was interdicted by Monarchs but it defied the law; it was fulminated against by prelates, but survived the onslaught; it was attacked by pens of the writers, but it has outlived them all.[2]

British Information Services

WEMBLEY CUP FINAL, ENGLAND

  With the revival of athletics after the Puritan epoch soccer football came back with a tremendous surge. It was adopted and modified by the English schools to meet their limited space for exercise. This limitation of space plus the need for decreasing injuries lead to the evolution of the dribbling game of today. From the schools it spread to the colleges of Oxford and Cambridge. J. C. Thring in 1862 drew up the first set of rules, which were ten in number and are still a part of the International soccer rules although some have been modified. In 1863, at a meeting in London of representatives of various organized teams, the "Football Association" was formed. This association adopted Thring's code of rules. Teams playing under these rules became known as Association Football teams, and from this the name of the game gradually changed from football to association football. The shorter name of soccer, which probably originated from the players' wearing socks, is commonly used in this country to distinguish association football from American football.

  From the British Isles the game spread to the other countries of Europe and to all the English colonies. Previous to 1930 forty Football Associations had been founded in nations all over the globe. At the present time soccer is played in more than

[2] Jeffrey, Bill, *The Boys with the Educated Feet;* Burgess Publishing Co., 1933, p. 1.

ninety-five countries, and it can be truly said that the sun never sets on the game of soccer. In most of these countries it is the national and most popular team game. Crowds of 100,000 or more people at a single match are not uncommon in the British Isles and South America. In 1904, the Federation Internationale de Football Association was formed in Paris for the purpose of governing the National Associations. One outcome of the Federation has been the unification of rules, so that now all countries play under the same code. It is possible for a traveling team to readily secure matches in any part of the world, as the game is played everywhere under the same rules.

The Federation Internationale de Football Association has 82 member nations. Because the Olympic Games cannot handle the number of teams desiring to compete, world-wide, geographical elimination tournaments are held to decide the teams allowed to enter the games.

Some form of soccer was being played in the American colleges as early as 1830, although the rules, if any, varied with different colleges. By 1860 many of the colleges along the Atlantic coast were playing soccer regularly and using about the same rules. In 1868, Rutgers and Princeton Universities formed a set of rules providing for 25 men on each team and six goals to constitute a game; i.e., the first team to score six goals should be declared the winning team. They specified also that the ball was to be kicked and not carried or thrown. The first intercollegiate game was played under these rules between teams representing Rutgers and Princeton at New Brunswick, N.J., on November 13, 1869. In this first game Rutgers was the first to score six goals and so won the game six to four. A week later in a return match Princeton won six to nothing.

Matches between other colleges were played during the succeeding years, but as each team had its own set of rules, there had to be compromises. Some of the colleges favored carrying the ball as well as kicking it (Rugby), while others were opposed to having the ball advanced by any other means than the feet (soccer). The mixup on rules and the bickering it caused between exponents of these two types of games led to the forming of the Intercollegiate Association Football (soccer) League in 1907. This association functioned until 1925. In 1926 an organization to take its place was formed and is now known as the Intercollegiate Soccer Football Association of America. It has a membership of about 127 colleges and universities.

The United States Football Association was founded in 1913 and immediately affiliated itself with the Federation Internationale de Football Association, the Amateur Athletic Union of the United States, and the American Olympic Association. It has affiliated with it over thirty-three organizations and two hundred soccer leagues. Two nationwide competitions are held in the United States every year: the National Challenge Cup Competition, which is open to both amateur and professional teams, and the National Amateur Challenge Cup Competition, open to amateur teams only. Teams compete for these cups in elimination matches, and interest and competition are keen. Soccer referees have organizations of their own as a part of the United States Football Association.

The first organization of soccer coaches was formed in New York in January, 1941. Known as the National Soccer Coaches Association of America, its purpose is the promotion and spreading of knowledge of the game.

The first National Collegiate Athletic Association national championship tournament was held in 1959. Eight teams, representing all sections of the United States, competed, with St. Louis University emerging as the champion. This soccer tournament is now one of the fifteen national championship competitions sponsored by the NCAA.

Soccer is growing in the United States but still has a long way to go to reach the popularity that it enjoys in other countries. It is estimated that the United States has 717 club teams with 14,340 players and that 167 colleges have teams with 9,000 players. When this is compared with the estimated 250 million soccer players in the world it appears insignificant. Soviet Russia has over a million and a half licensed soccer players, Germany over a million, and England over three-quarters of a million.

The number of public and private schools that afford the opportunity for playing soccer is hard to estimate. In general, it is popular in and around industrial cities. This can mostly be attributed to the immigrants who brought the game here from their native countries.

Soccer is growing in all parts of the United States because of the demand created on the high school athletic program for more sports, resulting from increased enrollment in the schools. In many sections of the United States school soccer is retarded only because of a lack of coaches and officials. This need not be, however, for the National Soccer Coaches Association and the United States Soccer Football Association both are willing to help and provide instruction to any organized group requesting such help.

CHAPTER II

Facilities, Equipment and Safety Suggestions

FACILITIES

Fields

The ideal field for the international game is either 120 yards by 75, or 110 by 65. The advantage of the bigger field is that it allows for more open play and demands more accurate passing and handling of the ball. The minimum dimensions of an intercollegiate field, according to rule, are 100 yards by 55 yards, but every effort should be made to get as near the maximum dimensions as possible. The ideal surface is a level and flat field of turf. Few prep or high schools have this ideal field and so get along with what they have. The rules do not specify any particular surface. Markings of the field should be according to the diagram in the National Collegiate Soccer Guide. The lines should be marked with wet lime on a grass field and with dry lime on a dirt field. If it is necessary to use dry lime on turf it is best that it be marked out while the dew is still on the grass. Wet lime cannot be satisfactorily put on a dirt field if the dust is heavy or if the field is very wet.

For eight-man soccer or for class work, fields may be arranged across the regulation soccer field.

To avoid a confusing number of white lines on the varsity field, the cross fields may be marked out with colored lime. Wet lime can be colored easily by adding powdered water color, which is cheap, and adds little to maintenance cost.

Goals

Goals, according to intercollegiate rules, shall be made out of 4" x 4" or 4" x 5" wooden posts with inside dimensions of 8 feet from ground to cross-bar and 24 feet between posts. Goal posts, may be made more durable by creosoting that part of the post which is set in the ground or by setting the posts in concrete. The ideal cross-bar may be secured by casing a 3" eye beam with wood, thus eliminating the sag that is often seen when all-wood cross-bars are used. The goals may be painted with white paint or with aluminum paint. Aluminum paint has the advantage of looking white and holding its color, while white paint has a tendency to lose its whiteness.

A suitable substitute for the cased steel cross-bar is made by bolting 2" x 5" planks together. If this is used it should be attached to the posts in such a way that from time to time it can be turned over to prevent too great a sag from developing. The goal nets should be supported by a pipe or wooden frame. A concave or a perpendicular net has the advantage that in practice the balls are easily retrieved from the net without the risk of tearing it.

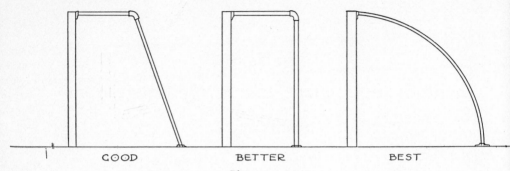

GOOD   BETTER   BEST

Pipe net supports.

The net should be fastened to the back of the uprights and cross-bar by means of hooks making it easy to put up or take down. Half-inch screw-eyes opened up to make a hook, placed twelve inches apart, make a very satisfactory arrangement. If a framework to hold a net is not possible the net may be pegged straight back or over a support.

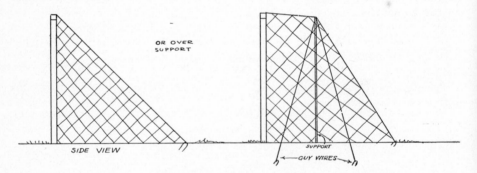

OR OVER SUPPORT

SIDE VIEW

SUPPORT

GUY WIRES

Simple methods of supporting nets.

When the net is pulled too tightly it gives resistance to the ball and is likely to tear.

Provided nets cannot be secured, it is better to use poultry wire than it is to play without any kind of net. For class work, makeshift goals may be made from light uprights, using a rope or sapling as a cross-bar and no nets.

Movable Goals

Movable goals should be made as light as possible so that they can be easily moved. The lightest material is wood. The next best material is two inch pipe. The disadvantage of pipe is that if it is bent, it is very difficult to straighten.

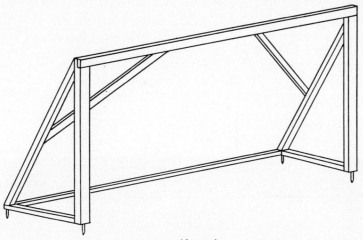

Movable goal.

The advantage of having movable goals is that they can be moved from place to place for practice; this saves the turf on the playing field and in front of the permanent goals. Another advantage is that they can be moved onto the regular field to make the regular field of the same dimensions as that of the opponents whom you next play away from home.

Corner Flags

Corner flags should be set in sockets at the four corners of the field. These sockets may be made of 2 inch pipe, 12 inches or more in length, set flush with the ground. The staff holding the corner flag should be made of wood that is pliable. Wood that is brittle is likely to snap off if hit by a player, and the piece remaining in the ground may injure him. Old bamboo vaulting poles make good flag staffs. According to rules the flag-staff shall not be less than five feet high. A substitute which is acceptable is a sapling, or a spring such as is used to hold the corner flags on football fields. The flag itself should be of some bright color, of any shape, approximately two feet long and one foot wide, made of some light material so that it will fly away from the staff in the slightest breeze.

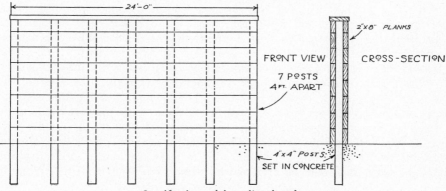

Specifications of bounding board.

Bounding Boards

Bounding boards are a great help to the coach but are not absolutely necessary Their advantage is that many types of kicks, games and targets can be used to stimulate the interest of the players. Where possible the bounding board should be so erected that it can be used from two sides. This will eliminate the time lost by chasing the balls that miss the bounding board. Those using the other side of the board may retrieve them. Where bounding boards must be placed on the edge of the field it is best to have them against a bank which will stop wild kicks. Bounding boards should be 8 feet high and 24 feet long.

Instep kicking practice on bounding boards.

EQUIPMENT

The most important part of a player's equipment is his shoes. The uppers of the shoe should be of soft leather cut low in back to permit proper extension of the ankle. A low box toe on a shoe is much to be preferred to a high box toe. A shoe built with straps on the sides which will pull up tight to support the arch of the foot is a great help in making the shoe feel comfortable. Shoes with removable, screw-in cleats are easier to keep in repair than are shoes that have nailed-on cleats. Another advantage of the screw-in cleat is that it does not tear the sole of the shoe when it pulls out. Nail-on cleats damage the shoe by pulling off part of the sole when they are scuffed off. Bakelite and rubber cleats are much less dangerous than the nailed-on cleat. If the leather of the nailed on cleat becomes worn down, the nails protrude. In general, cloth laces are better than rawhide laces as they will not stretch or shrink as much with changes in the weather.

A pair of soccer shoes can be made to fit perfectly when stock size does not seem to suit the player, by soaking the shoes. The method of doing this is to put on a pair of soccer shoes that feel small, lace them up fairly tight, and stand in hot water for fifteen or twenty minutes. The pressure of the foot against the inside of the shoe will cause the leather to shape itself to the form of the foot. The shoe should then be taken off, dried, and oiled to make the leather soft and pliable. A light soccer shoe is to be preferred to a heavy one as it tends to increase the

speed of the players. In Naval Aviation soccer because of the large numbers involved, rubber soled sneakers, basketball shoes, and 6 man soccer shoes have been
found to be satisfactory.

The next most important piece of equipment is the shin guard. The best type
of shin guard is molded out of plastic and is in one piece. This type of shin guard
will distribute the blow to the whole leg, whereas the reed type of shin guard
will not. The shin guard should be equipped with web cross-straps on the inside to
prevent the shin guard from coming into contact with the shin. Provided no shin
guards are available some protection will be afforded by a substitute fashioned from a
piece of a cardboard packing box.

Proper Equipment.

In order to allow for free circulation of the blood, the shin guard should be
held in place by the stocking rather than tied around the leg with tape. A dis-
tinguishing band of color low on the stocking enables the players in the game
to distinguish their own teammates without looking up. They should be woolen
and also footless, for footless stockings are easier to keep clean and can be worn
for a longer time than stockings with feet. A few long footless cotton stockings
should be bought to wear under the woolen stockings by the players whose skin
is irritated by wool.

Soccer balls have gone through such a rapid change in style that it is hard to specify which is the most satisfactory type. The leather covered laceless ball seems to be the most popular type as it tends to hold its shape better. Having no bulge caused by a lacer it will give a true bounce, and danger of being cut while heading is eliminated. The leather in the ball should be soft. If it is necessary to buy a cheaper one, an unofficial rubber ball will answer the purpose for class soccer. It has the advantage that on a rainy day it will not get heavy, and will stand a lot of abuse.

The above named equipment is the most important and is all that is absolutely required for intercollegiate soccer. Some items of equipment that are nice to have but not absolutely necessary are:

Soccer player dressed for action.

Soccer shorts should have a bell shaped bottom in the leg to allow for freedom of movement and should extend at least half way from the hip to the knee. An elastic waist allows the trunk muscles freedom of movement and is superior to any belt.

Soccer jerseys may be made of light worsted with full sleeves and a collar, with vertical contrasting stripes, fastened in front with a zipper or laced with tape. The goalkeeper should wear a jersey that is distinctly different from the team shirt, in order that the referee can easily distinguish the one allowed to handle the ball.

A baseball cap to shade the goalkeeper's eyes when playing against the sun.

A portable blackboard or miniature field board for lecture and discussion.
First Aid kit.
A shrill referee's whistle, a timer's horn, and *a timer* that can be stopped and started again.
Wire brushes for cleaning mud from shoes and balls. Oil and a ball cleaner for cleaning shoes and balls. Shoe lasts and shoemaker's hammer and pliers if leather cleats are used.
The equipment for intramural soccer or *class work* is very simple. Gym suits and basketball shoes are all that is necessary. Reversible jerseys with contrasting colors make it easy to distinguish the teams. Provided these are not available, colored sleeveless shirts of a bright color pulled over the regular gym jersey, or colored ribbons worn over the shoulder will serve this purpose.

Care of Soccer Balls

Soccer balls will last longer if they are given good care. If the leather cover looks dry, it should be washed with saddle soap and have applied to it a light, uniform coat of water-proofing. If the balls have been used on a wet day, the mud should be removed and the balls properly inflated before they are allowed to dry. The balls should be inflated to twelve pounds as required by the rules. At the close of the season the balls that are in good condition should be deflated to about half normal pressure and stored where they will not become folded or crushed. The balls that are in poor condition should be sent to some reliable cleaning company for repairs, reconditioning and new bladders. There are many firms that do this work excellently and it is much cheaper to have the balls reconditioned than to buy new ones.

SAFETY SUGGESTIONS

Shoes properly laced.—The shoe should be laced firmly to the foot, and if the shoe has no support for the instep, the shoe laces should be wrapped around the instep and then tied behind the ankle.

All cleats should be on the shoes and in good condition.

Players with weak ankles should have them taped or wrapped. Care should be exercised in the taping so as not to interfere with the extension of the foot.

There should be no metal ends on the laces that close the neck of the jersey. These metal ends are likely to fly up and injure the player's eye while he is running.

On a cold day olive oil or similar substitute rubbed on players' legs will help keep them from becoming cold and will help eliminate the danger of strained muscles. The players on the bench should be equipped with sweat pants and hoods.

A preparation to toughen the skin on the bottom of the feet should be used during the first few weeks of practice. This will help to eliminate blisters. As a good many blisters occur on the back of the heel because of the stiffness of the shoe, it is well to run a strip of adhesive tape up the back of the heel as a preventive measure. A good many soccer players like to use two pairs of socks, which will also help to prevent blisters.

Other factors which may be classed as safety measures are:

1. A well-controlled and well-officiated game.
2. Making the players report to the trainer all blisters, scratches and bruises.
3. Shin guards.
4. Metal cup supporters.
5. Cleared area beyond the edges of the field.
6. No holes in the field.
7. Do not allow some players to wear soccer shoes and others basketball shoes in the same game.
8. When a lace ball is used be sure the end of lacer does not show.
9. Tie shoe laces behind ankle; it helps prevent tripping over ends of laces. When tied in front the ball may not leave the foot accurately off the knot and the ball hitting the knot may cause a bruise on the top of the foot.

CHAPTER III

Warm-up Periods

In general the purpose of a warm-up period before instruction or a game, is to increase the circulation of blood, and to increase the suppleness of the body so as to insure maximum freedom of motion in the joints.

There are two methods which may be used to warm-up the players.

Warm-up Period Before Instruction

The first of these is mass exercises. Their advantage is that each player on the squad gets the same amount of exercise and the coach can be sure that all are warmed-up. The best exercises to use would be those of the following types, as they accomplish more than one purpose:

Exercises to strengthen the abdominal muscles.—These muscles are used in kicking and are more often under-developed than well-developed.

1. Lie on back and lift trunk or legs.
2. Crouch sitting to stoop falling.
3. Walking on all fours (hands and feet).

Exercises that will stretch the ham strings.—These muscles are used in running and if not stretched tend to limit the action of the knee joint.

1. Trunk bending forward from wide stride position with knees straight.
2. Sitting in a hurdle position and reaching for the forward leg with the opposite arm.
3. High kicking.

Exercises that will strengthen the arms, neck, and shoulder muscles.—The arm and shoulder muscles are used in running and throwing, and the neck muscles in heading.

1. Push-ups.
2. Head stand.
3. Lying on stomach with arms and legs raised backward and rocking back and forth.

Exercises that will teach falling in a relaxed and proper way.—The player that is knocked down will seldom be injured if he knows how to relax when falling.

1. Forward roll.
2. Forward roll over one shoulder.
3. Backward rolls.

Mass exercises should not be prolonged beyond the purpose of the warm-up period, or to the point where fatigue sets in. If the players are to receive the utmost value from them, they must be told why the exercises are given. In other words, they must understand the value of these exercises.

The second is by using the practice of fundamentals to warm-up. As the practice of skills without opposition is a mild form of exercise, it can be used without danger of straining muscles or pulling tendons.

1. Give fundamentals to practice, such as head, pass on run, head and **trap**, dribble, halves throw in and forwards' trap.

Warm-up.

2. Ball control drill. The ball control drill consists of trying to keep the ball in the air by playing it after each bounce. Its primary function is to loosen the ankle and develop facility in handling the ball with either foot.

3. Mass warm-up drill.

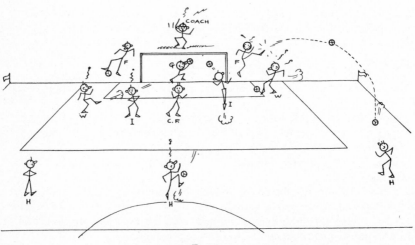

Fig. 1.

Goal tender retrieves each ball from net and punts or throws toward center of field. Fullbacks retrieve each ball that miss goal. Halfbacks trap ball, then either (1) set the ball up for a place kick or pass, (2) take a short dribble and set ball up or pass or, (3) cause ball to bounce so as to practice a pass or set-up from a volley or half-volley.

Have the halfbacks call out the name of the player he is passing to before he makes the pass, otherwise the back may merely be kicking the ball in an aimless fashion and not trying to place it.

If the coach stands behind the goal net he is in a safe position with all players in front of him. From here he can easily call out mistakes and make corrections.

Warm-up Period Before a Game

The warm-up before a game should be planned by the coach. The team should be instructed in the things which they are to do. The drill illustrated in Fig. 1 may be used as a practice warm-up. Each man should also practice the special duties which he is called upon to perform in the game, such as:

1. Wings taking corner kicks.
2. Center forward taking penalty kicks.
3. Halfbacks throwing the ball.
4. Goal keeper advancing the ball and dodging.
5. Fullbacks taking goal kicks.

When the game warm-up period is not planned, the team will usually all shoot goals or mill around in aimless fashion.

CHAPTER IV
Individual Fundamentals

Place a beginner and your best man side by side and look at them. They may be the same height and weight, have the same intelligence, speed, endurance and agility, have the same knowledge of the game, and yet as players they are not equal. One is a good player and the other is a poor player, because of their unequal ability to control the ball.

Ball control is the ability to get the ball in your possession and to do with it exactly as you desire without loss of time or motion. Ball control is the finished product, the completed whole, and is composed of many skills.

The purpose of this chapter is to set forth the "form" of the many skills, which, when all combined, are summed up in the term "ball control." There is a certain method of performing specific skills, which is known as "form." Form could be defined as the popular opinion of experts based upon body mechanics and the manner which seems to produce the best results in the majority of cases. However, it does not take into consideration the fact that individuals differ one from the other. If a player can produce results with an unorthodox form, there is no reason to attempt to change his style to meet the standard pattern.

The first step in teaching a skill is to present it in the proper form. This standard method of performing a skill could be called the pure fundamental, as no factors other than the simple movements are involved. In presenting a new skill the coach should give the players a mental image of how it is performed. This can be done by means of pictures, diagrams, word descriptions and demonstrations. If the coach is

Chalk talk.

18

to demonstrate it, he should do so in slow motion, for this will give the players a clearer picture of the technique involved. A coach should never try to demonstrate a fundamental with speed or against opposition unless he is certain that he can do it better than any player on the squad. The next step in presenting a fundamental is to explain its importance and relationship to the game as a whole. The coach may stress its importance by relating experiences of its use in actual game situations and how expert skill resulted in winning games. If the players realize its value, they will try hard to acquire the skill.

The second step is to practice the fundamental. The players should go through the motions involved in slow motion until they have mastered the correct form. The skill is then practiced with increasing speed, always being sure that correct form accompanies the accelerated movement. The coach should allow the player to learn as rapidly as his ability permits.

As a skill is not learned until it becomes the player's habit in a game, the third step is to teach this fundamental in an actual game situation. The coach should have the player practice when and where to use the skill by setting up situations which will arise in a game and will call for its use. These situations will usually call for opposition. The opposition should at first be as little as possible and gradually be increased to the point where the opposition is strong and aggressive.

Everyone realizes that while "practice makes perfect" it is more fun to play the game than to practice the fundamentals, and that continuous practice of skills gets monotonous after the skill is almost mastered or the newness of it has worn off. Lack of player interest in fundamentals is one of the things that all coaches contend with at some time or other. To keep player interest at a high peak the skills to be reviewed may be camouflaged by using them in competitive drills or games.

Most kicks are supposed to be made to a teammate; therefore, they are potentially all passes. As long kicks provide the opponents with a good chance for interception, which short kicks do not, they might or might not be passes. In this chapter kicks for whatever purpose they are used will be classed as long and short kicks.

LONG KICKS

Probably the most important kick of all, and certainly the hardest to coach and to learn, is the instep kick. Without some skill in using this kick a player is of little value to his team. Players could almost be rated as to their value to the team by their ability to make instep kicks. There are two variations from the simple instep kick; the outside-of-the-foot kick and the pivot instep kick.

Simple Instep Kick

Place the non-kicking foot alongside the ball. Swing the kicking leg forward from the hip and at the same time bend the knee so that the heel is well back. When the knee comes in line with the ball and the eye, straighten the leg. The top of the instep or shoelace should meet the ball, the toe being extended or pointed downward. The body should be over the ball. The power of the kick comes from the knee joint, not the hip, and is almost in direct relationship to the preparatory bend of the knee. The muscles of the leg should be relaxed until the kick is started, and the ankle at the moment of impact with the ball. The toe does not come into contact with the ball. A simple instep kick will have a backspin and will remain low in flight.

Simple Instep Kick. (a) Jump to non-kicking foot; (b) Non-kicking foot alongside of ball; (c) Eye, knee and ball in line at moment of contact; (d) Follow through of leg and body.

Stress:

Kicking leg relaxed.
Knee pointed forward.
Body over the ball.
Ankle relaxed.
Eye on ball—very important.
Jump to non-kicking foot as other leg swings into position for the kick. Have player practice the jump without a ball.

Uses:

On a still (non-moving) ball such as goal, penalty, and free kicks, where a long, low ball is desired.
When ball is coming toward you and you desire to return it in the same direction.
When a ball is approaching from behind and you wish to keep it going in the same direction.
When shooting for a goal.
When ball is rolling along in front of you and going in the same direction.

Outside of Foot Kick

The kick is made in the same manner as the simple instep kick except that the toe of the kicking foot is turned in. The ball meets the foot about on the small toe. When

Instep kick with outside of foot. (Note: the foot is turned in to meet the ball about on the small toe.)

the right foot is used for kicking, the ball may be met slightly to the left of or on the center axis. When the kick is mastered, it will result in a fast, low curved ball with a sideward spin.

Stress:

Kicking leg relaxed.
Knee pointed forward.
Body over the ball.
Ankle relaxed.
Eye on ball.
Jump to non-kicking foot as other leg swings into position for the kick. Have
the player practice without a ball.

Uses:

In place of simple instep kick.
To kick the ball on other than the center axis.
In shooting for goal by the center or inside forwards.
On corner kicks by the right wing with right foot to curve ball toward the goal
or with left foot to curve ball away from the goal.
By left wing on corner kicks with reverse results.

Pivot Instep Kick

The non-kicking foot should be placed from twelve to eighteen inches behind the
ball and to the same side of the ball as the direction in which it is to be kicked. The
action of the kicking leg is the same as for the simple instep kick, except that from
the hip the leg is swung in a circular sweeping motion. The body should lean slightly
backward and in the direction in which the ball is to be kicked. The more the body
leans, the nearer to the ball the non-kicking foot should be placed. The body pivots
on the non-kicking toe from the time that the foot meets the ball until the ball leaves
the foot in the new direction. The ball will normally follow the direction in which
the kicking foot points at the end of the follow through.

The technique of the instep kick and its two variations has been described for the
low, hard kick. It is not always desirable to make a kick of this kind, as there are
times when the ball should be lofted over the opponent's head. This can be done
with the simple instep kick or the outside-of-the-foot kick by meeting the ball in
front of, rather than under the body. A like result can be accomplished with the
pivot kick by meeting the ball under its center and nearer the toe of the shoe. If the
ball is being topped, the non-kicking foot is being placed too near the ball or the
body is not leaning. If the ball is hitting on the inside of the foot, the knee is being
turned out or is not following the body on the pivot.

Stress:

Kicking leg relaxed.
Eye on ball.
Lean forward to keep the ball low.
Lean backward to loft the ball.
Foot cupped around the ball.
Jump to non-kicking foot as other leg swings into kicking position.
Do not run around the ball.
Place the non-kicking foot to the side of the ball.

Pivot Instep Kick: (a) Body leaning in direction ball is to be kicked; (b) Foot swinging in short arc; (c) Pivot starts as foot meets ball; (d) Follow through well balanced.

Uses:

> To kick a ball on the side axis so as to send it in a direction other than that in which it is coming.
>
> On corner, penalty, and free kicks.
>
> To center the ball.
>
> For long passes (over 15 yards).
>
> For long or short shots at the goal.

Volley Kick

To volley-kick a ball is to kick it while it is in the air either before or after it bounces. The leg is swung from the hip, but the power of the kick comes from the knee joint and the follow through of the body. The ball is hit with the instep. The success of the kick depends almost entirely upon keeping the eye on the ball until it

Volley Kick: (a) Leg Swinging forward to bring knee over ball; (b) Knee over ball as kick starts.

meets the foot. The player should keep his eyes on the foot after the kick is made to get in the habit of watching the foot meet the ball. If the ball is to be kept low, it must be met as it nears the ground. A ball met waist high will be skied. Beginners have a tendency to get into position for the kick too soon, and consequently misjudge the flight of the ball. The player must be ready to change his stance until the last second. If shooting for goal, get the knee over the ball before straightening the leg. To get a long kick put the body into it by pushing off the non-kicking foot.

In an emergency the knee may be used to volley the ball. The weakness of the knee kick is that the ball is usually skied and not much power can be imparted. If the player finds himself in such a predicament, i.e., that the ball is coming too high for him to use the volley kick, he can overcome this by means of a jump-volley kick, which is a better kick than the knee-kick. It consists of jumping into the air off both feet and making the volley kick from this position. A hitch-kick may be used instead of a volley-kick and will give more distance. It consists of a jump with a scissors movement of the legs in front of the body. The non-kicking leg is swung into the air to aid the body in getting height. The legs are then quickly reversed as the kicking leg meets the ball. If used with players near, it is a *dangerous play* and a foul. For this reason many coaches discourage its use.

SCISSORS VOLLEY   KNEE VOLLEY   JUMP VOLLEY

The hardest ball to volley is the bouncing ball. Because of irregularities of the field, the ball may not bounce true, making it very difficult for the player to time his kick. If he kicks the ball as it is ascending, invariably it will be skied. He should meet it as it descends and preferably a few inches off the ground to obtain a low flight. The player should judge the bounce of the ball and then go in fast to make the kick.

Stress:
Watch the ball until it meets the foot.
Get the knee over the ball.
Wait until the last minute to get set for the kick.
Keep the body well balanced.

Uses:
To kick a ball on its under side.
To shoot for goal.
By backs to set the ball up in front of goal.
To clear the goal.

Half-Volley Kick (Drop-Kick Goalkeeper)

When a ball is kicked the instant after it hits the ground, it is called a half-volley kick. The ball is hit with an instep kick and results in a long, low ball.

Stress:

> Kicking leg relaxed.
> Knee pointed forward.
> Body over the ball.
> Ankle relaxed.
> Eye on ball.
> Emphasize eye on ball until foot makes
> contact.

Uses:

> By goalkeeper as it is a better kick than
> the punt because of its lower flight.
> By backs to clear goal or set up ball in
> front of opponent's goal.
> By forwards on bounding balls to shoot
> for goal or make long passes.

Over-Head Kick (Long)

The non-kicking foot is placed almost at leg's reach distance from the ball. The kicking foot meets the ball with the instep. The toe of the foot is flexed as soon as the foot meets the ball and remains flexed on the follow-through. The body leans backward away from the ball, enabling the leg to come through higher and removing the possibility of the player's own body blocking the kick. The leg is almost straight at the time the foot meets the ball.

Stress:

> Eye on ball until the foot meets it.
> Lean away from ball.
> Toe flexed.

Uses (when ball is in air):

> By any player to send ball in opposite
> direction from which he is facing.
> By backs to gain time in which to organize their defense, when the ball has
> been played over their heads and is
> bouncing toward their goal. In this
> case the placement of the ball is not
> so important as the power of the
> kick.

Half Volley Kick: (a) Eye on ball; (b) Body forward and well balanced; (c) Ball is met under the body.

Long Overhead Kick: (a) Illustrates the non-kicking foot is leg's distance from the ball, the body is balanced and the knee is bent; (b) Body leans backward and the toe is flexed on follow through.

Punt

See goalkeeper's skills.

Choosing the Kick

It is difficult for beginning players to choose the correct type of kick to use unless the coach points out to them the principle of the angle of rebounce. Use a wall to demonstrate the principle of the angle rebound of the ball. By throwing a ball against the wall, the coach can give the players a clear picture of where the ball will go when it hits or is kicked on its horizontal axis.

For example:

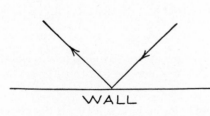

A ball coming from the right, if kicked on its center axis, will go to the left, as **the foot acts the same as a wall.**

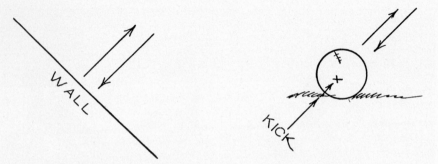

If a ball is kicked on its left axis, it will rebound to the right.

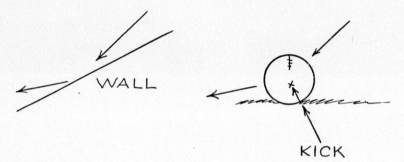

If a ball is kicked on the right axis, it will go to extreme left.

A ball coming straight toward a player will go back in the same direction if kicked on the center axis.

Therefore, the direction from which the ball is coming and the direction in which the ball should be kicked will determine the axis at which the foot should meet the ball.

The simple instep kick will enable the player to hit the ball on the center axis. The two variations of this kick enable him to meet the ball with his foot on the other two axes or any axis between the two extremes.

SHORT KICKS

The ability to impart just the correct amount of power to the ball calls for long hours of practice. As passes are in most cases made along the ground, the surface conditions of the field are an added and varying factor, making it important to practice passing in all kinds of weather and on rough and smooth turf and clay.

Inside of Foot (Push Pass)

The ball is met with the inside of the instep, or with that part of the foot between the big toe joint and the heel. The leg is swung from the hip, and the ball should be well under the body. If the ball is met in front of the body, the lower leg should be perpendicular to the ground. If the ball bounces, it is because it is being hit on the up-swing of the leg. This is probably the easiest short kick to coach and

Inside of foot pass. (Note: Pass to wing has been started. Lower leg is perpendicular to the ground to keep the ball from bouncing.)

to execute with accuracy. Its weakness is that the direction of the pass is obvious to the opponents, and therefore it should not be used where deception is necessary.

Stress:

Ankle relaxed.
Keep the ball on the ground. (Sweeping, follow through.)
Eye on ball as foot meets it.

Uses:

For accurate passes up to 15 yards.
For passing at any angle between sideward and forward.
For passes where deception is not needed.
For shooting for goal where accuracy is more desirable than power.

Inside-of-Foot Lob

The body must be well balanced on the non-kicking foot, and should lean toward the side of the kicking foot. The lower leg is at right angles to the upper

Lob pass (to a team-mate over an opponent's head): (a) Start of pass; (b) Ball makes contact; (c) Follow through of leg.

Outside of foot pass. (Note that by feinting to pass with the instep the opponent has been drawn out of positions.)

part of the leg. The force of the kick comes from the hip, with the inside of the foot meeting the ball.

Stress:

Use arms to keep balance.

Keep eye on ball until after the kick.

Keep knee bent. Practice for accuracy.

Uses:

For short pass over opponent's head by halfbacks to forwards.

For forwards as a means of getting the ball by the defense or beating the one marking them.

On throw-in plays.

Outside of Foot (Flick or Jab)

The kick is made by straightening the knee and swinging the leg away from the body. To raise the ball off the ground abduct the foot at the ankle joint as the outside of the instep meets the ball.

Stress:

Push the ball rather than kick it.

Use a feint before passing.

Eye on ball.

Uses:

For passes up to 15 yards.

In connection with deceptive dribbling and deceptive passing.

Sole of Foot

The sole of the shoe is placed lightly on the ball. The ball is rolled in a back-ward direction by a quick flexion of the knee. If the pass is made on a run, the player jumps and executes the movement while in the air. While this is not a kick it is a useful pass and an easy one for the receiver to handle.

Stress:

Place foot lightly on the ball.

Keep body well balanced.

Look for the receiver before passing.

Uses:

To pass backward.

By inside forward, to pass to wing on combination play "C." Page 153.

Heel

The heel of the kicking foot meets the ball as the leg is swung backward from the hip and the knee is flexed.

Stress:

Hit the ball on the center.

Know where you are passing.

Sole-of-Foot Pass: (a) Ready to jump and place foot on ball; (b) Foot lightly on the ball.

Uses:

To prevent ball from going over side or goal lines.

By a forward, to pass backward to a halfback after feinting a shot at goal.

Short Overhead

The ball is met on the instep slightly toward the toe by a sharp straightening of the knee and flexing of the ankle. The ball will have much back-spin if the kick is executed properly.

Stress:

The ball must meet the instep before the ankle is flexed.

The ball should be kept low, and only just over the head or shoulder.

Heel Kick. Shows heel starting to make backward kick.

Uses:

To "beat" an opponent.

By center or inside forwards to get ball behind the defense in front of goal.

As a pass to oneself.

Short overhead kick. (A kick used to get the ball behind the defensive players.)

PASSING

One pass is worth two kicks. If beginners have this impressed upon them, it will not take long before they have started to graduate from the beginners' class. There are three factors in a pass: the passer, the ball, and the receiver. If each one fulfills the necessary requirements, the result is perfect teamwork.

The Passer

Should conceal his intention until the last moment.
—not pass to a covered teammate.
—look up from the ball, so as to see the receiver, and then look down at the ball while making the kick.
—pass to an open spot in front of the receiver.
—if necessary, call name of receiver before making the pass.

The Ball

Should have correct amount of speed.
—be on the ground and not bouncing during passing.
—"lead" the receiver—too much lead can be overcome by more speed on the part of the receiver, but too little causes the receiver to slow up.

The Receiver

Should so place himself that he is in position to receive a pass. This means getting between the man marking him and the ball or starting into a clear place.
—come to meet the ball.
—keep eye on ball when receiving.
—take a quick look at the field of play as the ball is traveling toward him.
—instantly decide what he will do with the ball.
—run relaxed, with short strides to keep the body balance well under control. This will enable him to speed up or change direction to receive the pass.

TRAPPING

Trapping is to get control of a pass or a loose ball by stopping it or by changing its direction to suit your purpose. Much time must be spent on it by beginners, and advanced players should review it often. The coach should insist that all balls in practice be trapped or placed under control before they are played. The exceptions would be when practicing "first time" kicks. Except when clearing the goals, all players will play better soccer if they adopt the slogan—"Trap first, kick second." A ball is properly trapped when it stops "dead" at the foot or, when trapping by re-directing the ball, it remains within one step. This can be accomplished by using some soft part of the body to trap with, such as calf or thigh or abdomen, by keeping the leg limp when trapping with the foot, or, the most difficult, to trap the ball so it will rebound vertically. It should be constantly pointed out to the players that in all cases the trapping leg is off the ground and relaxed, and that the eye must watch the ball until it reaches the point of contact. Other methods of trapping have been purposely omitted either because they are more difficult to learn, or are seldom used. Players that can perfectly execute two types of traps for rolling, bounding, and fly balls will rarely need to practice any other methods

Body balance may not be a skill, but it is something that must be mastered by all soccer players. It is a necessary part of every kick or trap. Beginners should be encouraged to use their arms to maintain balance, either held sideward or forward.

Rolling-Ball Traps

With Sole of Foot

While facing the ball, raise the foot with the knee slightly bent and the toe higher than the heel, making a "V" between the sole and the ground into which

Sole of foot trap on rolling ball. (Ball rolls into "V" formed between foot and ground.)

the ball rolls. The weakness of this trap is that it leaves the trapper motionless and faced in the direction from which the ball is coming. This causes him to face before next playing the ball and consequently lose time.

Stress:

Leg extended.
Eye on ball in case of a bad last bounce.
Foot turned up to 45° angle.

Uses:

To trap a rolling ball.

With Side of Foot (Deflection)

The trapping foot is off the ground and turned so that as the ball meets the foot, it rebounds in the desired direction. The receiver should take a flash look to determine the position of the opponents as the ball comes to him. The players must learn this skill with the inside and the outside of each foot.

Stress:

Watch the ball hit the foot.
Lean in the direction the ball is to be deflected.

Deflection trap with outside of foot.

Trap ball at right angles to approaching opponents.

Uses:

By any player except goalkeeper.

BOUNDING-BALL TRAPS

With Sole of Foot

Same as for rolling-ball traps except that the leg is usually straight and the foot meets the ball just as it bounces from the ground. The body should at once move forward with a step on the trapping foot in order to place the ball under control.

Stress:

Bring the toe of the shoe down over the ball to finish the trap.

Face in the direction of the ball so that if the trap is missed with the foot, the body can be used.

Uses:

To trap a ball just as it hits the ground.

When any movement of the ball would give it to an opponent.

When it is not possible to come up to the ball to make a leg trap.

Bounding ball trap with sole of foot.

With Inside of Leg

The knee is at right angles to the oncoming ball. The foot is off the ground with the knee bent. The ball is played with the thigh or calf muscles.

Stress:

Leg must be kept relaxed.
Foot of trapping leg must be held off the ground.

Uses:

To trap or deflect a bounding ball in the air up to waist high.
On a ball coming from any sideward or forward direction.

Inside of leg trap. (Ball meets soft part of leg.)   *Stomach trap. (Trunk has started to bend over the ball.)*

With Inside of the Foot

Same as for relaxed leg except that ball meets the foot. The foot should be turned to deflect the ball in the direction the player is going to move.

Stress:

Foot held relaxed or allowed to give slightly to absorb the speed of the ball.

Uses:

On a low-bouncing ball coming from any sideward to forward direction.

With Stomach or Chest

If the player desires to bring the ball dead to his feet, he relaxes or bends forward at the waist as the ball hits. By moving forward as the ball hits, he can start it moving in the direction he is going to travel.

Stress:

Hold arms away from body as ball hits, or referees may suspect hand
trapping.
Keep relaxed.

Uses:

On a ball over waist high.

Relaxed chest trap. (To bring ball to feet.)

*Fly ball trap with sole of foot. (Note: Foot is
held over the ball and ball traps itself.)*

FLY-BALL TRAPS

With Sole of Foot

The knee is raised and the foot brought over the ball at the instant that it hits
the ground. The rebounding ball should hit the sole of the foot.

Stress:

Face the on-coming ball.
Do not get set too soon or the flight of the ball may be misjudged.
Foot does not hit ball.

Uses:

When there is ample time to trap before an opponent can reach you.
If the wind is strong.

Fly ball trap with inside of leg. (Illustrates trapping to the left with body starting to move in that direction.)

With Side of the Leg or Inside of the Foot

The leg moves so that the knee is pointed toward the ball, with the lower leg held slightly backward and outward. The ball is wedged between the inside of the leg and the ground at its moment of impact with the ground.

Stress:

The body should lean in the direction in which the ball is to be trapped.
Eye on the ball. Tendency is to look for the opponent.
Keep leg relaxed.
Do not get set too soon.

Uses:

To trap fly or low bounding balls.
To deflect fly balls.

DRIBBLING

Beginners tend to dribble too much and to maintain the dribble too long. A dribble is usually indicated if no opponents are near, and should be maintained until one of the defensive players has been drawn to the dribbler. The coach should point out to the players that a pass is a more dependable method of beating an opponent. The player is justified in trying to dribble by an opponent if there is no one to whom to pass the ball, or if he can set up a scoring play. The eyes should glance ahead to see a chance for a play but the head should not be raised.

With Inside of Foot

The ball is tapped, coaxed, pushed along the ground with the inside of the foot. The body should be forward, with the head over the ball. The feet usually alternate in playing the ball. The ball should travel in a straight line.

Stress:

> Keep the ball near the feet.
> Push, not kick the ball.
> Keep the ball traveling straight ahead.

Uses:

> To advance the ball under control.
> When an opponent is coming from a forward direction.
> When control is worth more than speed.

With Outside of Foot

The ball is pushed with the outside of the foot about at the small toe. To do this, the foot is turned in between steps. The ball is played by the same foot

Dribbling with outside of foot. (Shows right wing dribbling down the right side-line.)

with every second step; i.e., push ball with right and step right, step left, push ball with right and step right, etc.

Stress:

Look at the ball when the foot plays it.
Eyes up, but not the head, to see the field of play.
Change to inside of foot when meeting opposition.

Uses:

To keep the body between an opponent and the ball. For example, by the right wing with right foot to keep the body between opponent and the ball while going down the side line.
When a fast dribble is desired.

HEADING

The direction of the ball when headed will be chiefly governed by where the head makes contact on the ball. If the ball is met near the underside, the ball will go up; if it is hit near the horizontal axis, it will go down. It is easier to head the ball back up into the air and for this reason it should be taught first. The most useful one and the most difficult type of heading to master is to head the ball down.

From Forward to Forward Direction

The ball is hit by the top of the forehead. The eyes should follow the ball as long as possible. The feet should be off the ground and the ball met as high in the air as possible. Greater distance can be obtained by using the neck muscles. The head is brought back and then forcefully forward, hitting the ball with the

Heading the ball down. (Note the head has come forward to hit the ball.)

forehead while the chin is brought in. The head follows through as much as is possible by being stretched forward away from the shoulders.

Stress:

Hit the ball with the head rather than let it hit you.

Do not duck the head; see the ball hit.

Time the jump and the flight of the ball so that you meet it high in the air.

Take-off from one foot by driving from hip, knee and ankle joints with the body erect.

Do not attempt to head a ball below chin height.

Uses:

To move the ball to an unoccupied area where you can get control of it.

To shoot for goal.

To place the ball preferably at the *foot* of one of your teammates.

To clear the goal.

From Forward to Sideward Direction

The technique is the same as for forward heading except that the ball is hit with the side of the forehead. It is best to cock the head to one side before thrusting it against the ball. The head should follow through and finish near the opposite shoulder.

Stress:

Face the on-coming ball.

See also forward heading.

Uses:

See forward heading.

From Forward to Backward

An on-coming ball may be headed backward by letting it bounce off the top of the head when the ball has little force. A better method is to turn the side of the body to the on-coming ball and play the ball with the top of the forehead by using a head flick.

BALL CONTROL

"The ball works for the good player, while the poor player works for the ball."

This quotation is often heard when "old-timers" gather and start to discuss the ball control of various players. It means that the ability of some players to control the ball makes their performance seem so easy that the player himself does not seem to be exerting himself. Other players use twice as much energy and do not accomplish as much work. Due to their lack of ball control, they fumble their passes, heads, and traps, and consequently are continuously chasing the ball.

Ball control is not a skill itself but is the sum of the player's execution of all the skills. Some of the best drills and games are devoted to no particular skill but embody many, and therefore could be classed as developers of ball control.

Heading for Goal: (a) Facing the on-coming ball. (b) Getting off the ground. (c) Hitting with the side of the forehead. (d) Following through with the head. (e) Following through with the body. (f) Following up the shot.

TACKLING AND CHARGING

Tackling is an attempt to get the ball from an opponent and, in most cases, is accompanied by a charge. Charging is an attempt to use a part of the upper shoulder to unbalance the opponent in order to secure the ball. A player does not always gain possession of the ball when he tackles, and yet he has served well if he stops the dribble, makes the dribbler lose control of the ball, or forces him to make a poor pass. There is no excuse for often missing both the tackle and the charge and thus being beaten. One or the other should succeed in stopping the opponent. The tackle should be so made that if it is missed the opponent cannot cut in for the goal but will be forced toward the side line.

Tackling

There are times when a tackler should come in fast to make the tackle and other times when he should make a cautious approach or even give way by backing up. Which of these are used largely depends upon the skill of the opponent and the situation.

If the dribbler loses control of the ball momentarily or an opponent has not yet gained control of the ball, a tackle is not necessary. The ball should be hooked or pushed at right angles to the opponent's run. His momentum will carry him at least one step beyond the ball, which gives all the time necessary to recover it.

The slide tackle has been purposely omitted because it is so difficult to execute without committing a foul that it is not recommended.

Stress on All Tackling

Make the man with the ball lead, i.e., cause the ball to move.

Time your movements so that you tackle just after the dribbler has played the ball.

When the charge is used with the tackle:

Face the opponent.

Have your shoulder hit him just enough to make him lose his balance.

Make a light charge, well timed.

The Two-Leg Tackle

Get both feet in front of the ball with the heels almost together, the knees turned out, and the body leaning forward. The ball is trapped by the legs while the shoulder charges the opponent off the ball. Follow up the tackle by stepping forward with one foot and pulling the ball along with the other. If the charge is with the right shoulder, step with the left foot.

Stress:

Keep weight forward.

Uses:

From in front of an opponent and near the ball.

When the opponent is not ready to dodge the tackle or has not full control of the ball.

When the opponent has no room to dodge the tackle or is not expecting a tackle.

*Two-Leg Tackle: (a) Shows going in fast after opponent has played the ball. (b)
Player's weight is forward with arm of charging shoulder close to side.*

The One-Leg Tackle

The body lunges forward with the inside of the lunging foot against the ball
and the knee bent. The ball is trapped with this foot and lower leg. The other leg
is backward to brace the body as the shoulder charge is delivered. Following the
charge this leg steps forward, while the ball is pulled forward by the trapping
foot. If the tackle is made with the right foot, the right shoulder delivers the charge.

Stress:

Do not cross-body block the opponent.
Face the opponent.

Uses:

From in front or diagonally in front of an opponent.
To stop an opponent's dribble.
To force an opponent to pass or to lose control of the ball.

The Sole-of-the-Foot Tackle

Place the sole of the foot on the ball with the leg straight out in front as the
opponent starts to play it. The ball should be wedged between the ground and the
foot as in the sole-of-the-foot trap.

Stress:

Be directly in front of the ball.
Weight forward.
Body well balanced.

One-Leg Tackle: (a) Illustrates weight on lunging leg and shoulder making a light charge; (b) Note: left foot steps forward following the charge; (c) Pulling the ball forward with the trapping leg.

Uses:

From directly in front and near the opponent.
To prevent an opponent from gaining control of the ball.
To block a kick.

The Pivot Tackle

The same as for the one-leg tackle except that the body is turned toward the opponent by pivoting on the non-tackling foot. The degree of the pivot will depend upon the angle of approach. It is necessary to be ahead of the dribbler to allow time for the pivot.

Stress:

Do not tackle too soon or from too far away.

Uses:

To tackle while approaching from the side or diagonally from the side of an opponent.

CHARGING

The weight of the body is thrown against the opponent, making contact with the shoulder against, or slightly in front of his shoulder. When coming from behind the dribbler, run in step with him and make the charge as his farther foot steps on the ground. As the charge is made, the foot nearest the dribbler steps in toward the ball.

One-Foot Tackle. (Note: The ball is firmly held and is directly in front of the tackler.)

Charging. Step toward ball as charge is delivered.

The coach must be sure that his players understand the charging rule or they will make numerous fouls. The chief points of this rule are that the arm shall be close to the body, that the tip of the shoulder shall be used, that the arm and shoulder shall not be moved in making the charge, that both players have at least one foot on the ground, that the charge must not be violent, that it can be used only when attempting to play the ball, and then, *not from behind* unless the opponent is intentionally obstructing.

Stress:

Keep your charge high to avoid fouling
Keep arm close to body.
Do not hunch the shoulder.
Keep one foot on the ground.
Watch your opponent's feet.

Uses:

To come from behind a dribbler and make a tackle.
To unbalance an opponent as you strive with him for possession of the ball.
To put the goalkeeper in the net when he has the ball.

*Obstructing. (Note that the center halfback has retarded center forwards' progress
toward the ball.)*

OBSTRUCTING

A legal method of impeding the progress of an opponent is by remaining in the
path in which he desires to move. This can best be done by turning your back
to him and giving ground slowly forward while moving sideward to prevent his
going around you. By giving ground and turning away from your opponent you are
much less likely to be charged with illegal play. Remember that you can be fairly
charged from behind when obstructing.

Stress:

Avoid moving toward opponent. Give ground.
Keep on toes and well balanced.
Watch opponent over your shoulder.

Uses:

To prevent the opponents from rushing your goalkeeper on corner, penalty or close-in free kicks.

To slow up an opponent so that your goalkeeper can handle the ball.

To delay an opponent so that the ball may roll out over the side or end lines.

THROWING (International Rule)

The palms of the hands are on opposite sides of the ball with the fingers toward the back and gripping the ball firmly. The wrists are bent downward so that the ball is held well back of the head. The distance of the throw depends upon the explosive power or snap of the muscles used. The wrist, elbow, shoulder, and trunk all enter into the throw. At the time of throwing one foot should be ahead of the other to maintain the balance. If the ball has side-spin, it has probably been thrown over the shoulder and is an illegal throw. The thrower should conceal the direction of his throw until the last moment. This can be accomplished by facing the field of play squarely and pivoting on the toes or turning at the waist

Throwing: (a) Note the ball starts from behind the head, the wrists are flexed, and the body is bent backward; (b) The wrist, elbow, shoulder, and trunk muscles are all in action; (c) The wrists are following through and a part of each foot is on the ground.

just as the throw starts. The throw must lead the receiver if he is moving, and the thrower must decide whether to throw to the receiver's feet, head, or body. Too often the throws are made merely in the general direction of the receiver and thus are awkward to handle. A long throwing player can reach more of his teammates, thus spreading out the defense and giving the throw-in added importance. Wing forwards as well as wing halfbacks should receive practice in throwing.

Stress:

Start the ball from behind the head.

Keep part of each foot on the ground at the moment of throwing.

Do not lob the throw if throwing for short distances

Use:

To put the ball in play.

RUNNING

Running is not a fundamental and need not be practiced as a separate skill. But, as it enters into the game and much of a player's success depends upon it, the coach should look for and correct poor form. The form will vary according to the purpose of the run, but two factors should always be present. These are relaxation to save strength and body control to maintain balance.

The body can be relaxed when running to get into position or when not in the play. Every opportunity to rest should be taken. If players will learn to run at three-quarter speed, they will have some extra power in reserve. Extra speed will often enable them to beat an opponent to the ball. The long striding sprint with vigorous arm action should be conserved for the time when it is necessary.

When running and anticipating a pass, the body should be kept under control by using short steps with the weight on the balls of the feet. From such a run it is easy to change direction or to break into a sprint. Change of pace is important in soccer as in all sports. If a player is closely marked and expecting a pass, the speed should be moderate and the pace suddenly increased as the pass starts. Change of pace should gain for the player the one step necessary to reach the ball ahead of the opponent.

FEINTS AND PIVOTS

These might be called special abilities and most players tend to specialize on a few deceptions with which they have the greatest success. Feints are valuable tactics as they tend to confuse the opponents. Passes should be preceded by a feint if the receiver is likely to meet opposition. Again feints should be used to draw the passer's opposition off balance or out of position so that the pass can be gotten away. The means that may be used are:

Feinting with the knees in one direction and passing in the other. Used from a stride stand with the ball in front of and near the feet, feet astride and weight on the toes. Suddenly bend the knees, turning them slightly to the left and look left. The body weight is kept over the feet and the pass is made to the right.

Feinting to pass with the inside of the foot but stopping the foot before it hits the ball. It may be used on a still or a moving ball.

Feinting to pass with the inside of the foot by bringing the foot over the ball and then passing in the opposite direction with the outside of the foot. It is mostly used on a still ball or while dribbling with the insides of the feet.

Feinting an instep kick by passing the foot over the ball or stopping it before it meets the ball. The first mentioned is a good feint for a back-heel or sole-of-foot pass.

Feinting to kick or pass can be effectively combined with change of pace while dribbling to beat an opponent and continue the dribble. It is a good feint for wing forwards who usually have only one man to beat in order to get in the clear down the side lines. The dribbler should approach slowly with the ball under control. If he can cause the back to shift his balance momentarily toward the center of the field by feinting a kick or a pass, he can beat him by pushing a short pass to himself beyond the back and down the side line. In passing the back he should run with knees high to avoid being tripped by the back's belated attempt to tackle.

*Knee Feint to Left. Note opponent has been
feinted off balance.*

Feinting a kick or a pass may cause an opponent to shift to one side, and then a dribble may be started to the other side. Feinting may be used to beat an opponent when neither of the players are moving as when the man with the ball and the opponent have reached a stalemate.

The ability to dodge to either side of an on-coming opponent is a skill that all players should master. The dodge should be learned on a non-moving ball. The feet should be in a stride position with the ball between and slightly in front of them. Split-vision should be used to watch the on-coming opponent's feet as well as the ball. The dodge should be made to the left if the opponent will be stepping on the left foot when he is two strides away. By quickly pulling the ball to the left with the right foot and taking a long cross step in front of the left with the right foot both the ball and the body are out of the opponent's reach. The left foot should regain control of the ball. The faster the opponent approaches, the easier it is to dodge him, provided the ball is under control. When the opponent is coming from a diagonally forward direction, the ball must be played at right angles to his approach.

If an opponent is on you before you have time to dodge, the evasion dodge is worth trying. It consists of pushing the ball to one side of the opponent while you go to the other side and cut back to get the ball. Push the ball at right angles to the rushing opponent, jump quickly one step out of his way and if possible in the direction from which he is coming, and then go for the ball. The opponent's momentum should carry him out of the play. This is only a substitute for dodging and should be used only for that purpose. It is more dangerous, since you lose control of the ball for a moment.

Dodging: (a) Pulling the ball; (b) Cross-stepping; (c) Finishing the dodge.

Dribbling can be made deceptive and tackling more difficult for the opponent by:

1. *Swaying the body from side to side.*—It should be used only when approaching an opponent. Called weave dribbling, it is an exaggerated swaying of the body accompanied by a weave run. The dribble is changed from inside of foot to outside of foot, or as may best serve to keep the ball traveling in a straight line during the weave.

2. *Shifting the body from side to side by feinting changes of direction.*—The feet must be kept apart, almost at a stride position, while the body does the feinting. The player uses lunge steps to keep his body under control while mixing up diagonally forward skips, jumps, and change steps with his feet. The ball may travel in a straight line or in a series of straight lines. Shifting can be used in a combination with feinting kicks, passes or change of pace either to beat an opponent or to pull him out of position so as to get off a pass.

Deceptive Dribbling: (a) Swaying the body; (b) Using the arms for balancing; (c) Starting a feint. Note eyes are on the ball; (d) Lunging to recover from feint; (e) Recovering from feint; (f) Resuming dribble. Note that the body is over the ball; (g) Starting a weave movement; (h) Note that the ball has traveled in a straight line.

Dribbling past an opponent who is approaching slowly can be accomplished by watching his feet. The attempt to dribble by should be made to that side on which he has his foot when he is about three steps away.

A stalemate occurs when the player with the ball is stopped because an opponent is in front of him. If the man with the ball can cause the opponent to lead (make a movement toward the ball), he has a chance to go by him. If the opponent can make the player with the ball lead, then he has a good chance to make a successful tackle. Thus a feinting duel starts which, provided neither player is fooled, will force the man with the ball to make a pass. No feint or pivot will succeed when the opponent is more than one stride away from the ball and cannot be coaxed nearer or put off balance.

When two opponents approach from opposite directions as you are trapping, they may be beaten by playing the ball between them.

One opponent can be beaten by playing the ball beyond him as described under heading, inside-of-foot-lob, and short overhead kick. When the ball is on the ground, it can be played over his tackling leg or over his head by jabbing the foot under the ball and lifting with the toe of the foot.

FUNDAMENTAL SKILLS EVALUATED

All skills are important to each position, but some have more value then others in certain positions at the public school soccer team level. The fundamentals below are ranked in the order of their importance for each position, with the most valuable being designated by the numeral one. Where one is as valuable as another, equal ranks have been assigned; for example, in the inside forward position shooting, passing, tackling, and feinting are equal in rank, as they are of equal importance.

This chart will enable the school coach to place his players in the positions where they will be of the greatest value to the team, and will act as a guide in the allocation of practice time to each fundamental. For example, a fullback should spend much more of his practice time on tackling and clearing the goal than he does on

	Obstructing	Taking free kicks	Tackling	Long kicking	Charging	Trapping	Heading	Dodging	Kicking-in	Dribbling	Setting up ball	Feinting-Dodging	Passing	Pivot kicking	Shooting	Kicking corners	Kicking penalties
Fullbacks	7	8	1	1	3	4	5	6									
Halfbacks		10	1		9	1	7		8	6	1	1	1				
Outside forwards					8	7				1		5	3	1	6	4	
Inside forwards			1		5	7				5		1	1	8	1		
Center forwards			8		4	6				7		2	3		1		5

dodging, as the rank assigned to tackling and clearing the goal is one and the rank to dodging is six. Should a coach not have time to cover all skills, he should attempt to train his players well in those having the greatest value.

Back-heel pivot: (a) Jumping over the ball; (b) Pivoting; (c) Completing pivot; (d) Centering the ball.

A back-heel pivot is performed by jumping over a moving ball. The ball is stopped by rolling into the back of the heel. The other foot takes a long forward stride to check the body momentum, which is followed by an about-face on the toes. For example, if the right foot jumps over the ball, the ball is stopped by the right heel, the left leg lunges forward, and the turn is made to the right. It can be used as an opponent is running along with you to prevent him from charging you off the ball. The foot opposite the opponent should jump over the ball in this case to screen the ball. It can be used to reverse directions with the ball. It can be used by the left outside forward to enable him to center with the right foot in case this is his strongest foot.

Screen pivot: (a) Stepping over the ball to obstruct the opponent; (b) Pulling the ball with the sole of the foot; (c) Recovering the ball.

The screen pivot can be used to get the ball away from an opponent when at close quarters. It consists of stepping over the ball with one foot and pulling the ball to the side with the sole of the other foot as the body pivots around the opponent. It may be accompanied by a shoulder charge. If the right foot steps over the ball, as the body starts its turn the right shoulder makes contact with the opponent, and the ball is pulled to the right with the sole of the left foot as the body turns left. The left foot steps on the ground as the right foot regains the ball. When your foot steps over the ball, you screen the opponent's view and prevent him from reaching it.

An inside-of-the-foot trap and pivot can be used to good advantage by the center forward. It is used when the center forward is near the opponent's goal, facing his own goal, closely marked, and he is about to receive a pass. The player moves forward to meet the ball and is followed by his marker. The ball is trapped or guided between the legs with the inside of the foot farthest from the opponent as the body pivots on the opposite foot. To complete the pivot the trapping foot is placed on the ground and the pivoting foot plays the ball.

CHAPTER V

The Goalkeeper's Skills

The skills of the goalkeeper are so important that they should be considered by themselves. As his ability to defend his goal is often the difference between victory and defeat, it is important that he receive a fair share of the coach's time in practice. The fundamental skills of the goalkeeper are:

Stance

The weight should be well balanced on the balls of the feet, which should be parallel and a comfortable distance apart. The knees should be slightly bent. The

Stance.

hips should be back and the trunk leaning forward. The arms should be bent almost at right angles and relaxed, with the elbows back and sideward. The hands should be well out in front of the body with the palms facing forward. The head should be up, with the eyes *concentrating* on the ball. In changing position and maintaining a stance the body stays low. The technique of moving sideward is to widen the stride and then close it, i.e., in moving to the right the right foot moves sideward first and is quickly followed by the left. Under ordinary circumstances the stance should be taken approximately one yard out from the goal, and slightly to the shortest side of the angle of possible shot.

Anticipation

The goalkeeper should anticipate a shot by an opponent and get set to receive it. He can usually tell when an opponent is going to shoot by watching the ball and the player. He can sometimes tell in which direction the shot will go by watching the kicking leg. By attempting to anticipate the opponent's next play, the goalkeeper will in time develop the knack of always being in the proper place at the proper moment. Anticipation does not mean that he commits himself by moving to a new position, but means that he gets ready to do so. Whenever the goalkeeper leaves his goal, he should notify the fullbacks by some prearranged signal so that one of them will drop back and cover the goal.

Catching

The hands should be open, fingers comfortably apart, elbows close to the body and the wrists nearer together and finger tips of both hands farther apart than the diameter of the ball. The hands should be held well out in front of the body, but should start moving toward the body just before the ball meets them. The eyes should follow the ball until the catch is completed. The arms should be drawn back toward the body to absorb the momentum of the ball (a "liquid" catch). If the ball is given any resistance by the palms of the hands, it may rebound and cause a fumble. The body should be behind the hands to stop the ball in case the hands fail to hold it. The goalkeeper should be alert to catch free kicks and set-ups and to deflect or catch corner kicks and centers.

Catching a low ball. (Note: Knees are turned out.)

Fielding a rolling ball. (Showing body behind the ball.)

There are two methods of getting the body behind a foot to knee-high ball. The first of these is with the heels close together, bend the knees outward, reach down between the knees, catch the ball slightly underneath and guide it to the stomach. The second is to place the right foot slightly behind the left foot and kneel on the right with the knee turned away from the body. Catch the ball slightly below its horizontal axis and guide it to the stomach. If it is necessary to move sideward in order to get in front of the ball and there is not time to use either of these two methods, kneel with the knee turned toward the opposite foot and turn the trunk forward. For example: in going to the left for a "stop," kneel with the right knee toward the left foot and twist the body to the right.

Catching. (Showing method of kneeling when moving sideward for the ball.)

To get the body behind a knee to chest-high ball, if it is a slow bouncing or a lob ball, catch the ball slightly below its horizontal axis and bend the trunk forward as the ball is drawn in. If the ball is a fast one, take it with a "liquid" catch and bring it to the stomach.

If possible on a chest to head-high ball jump and take it as in previous method. If it is too high to bring to the stomach, be sure the chest is in back of the catch.

Catching a head-high ball. (Note: Ball has been taken with liquid catch and brought to the chest.)

When it is necessary to move sideward for a ball and impossible to get the body behind the catch, two hands should be used with the palms facing the ball, both thumbs behind the ball and touching each other. When the ball is beyond reach of both hands but near enough to catch with one hand, the catching hand on the back of the ball should be followed immediately with the second hand on the front of it.

Starting from a kneeling catch.

The goalkeeper should practice getting to his feet and starting fast from all the catches where he is required to kneel.

Stress:

Watch the ball and not the approaching players.
Play each ball as if the game depended on that one "stop."
No fumbling or careless catching during practice.
Practice with a wet ball and in the rain. Wear woolen gloves in wet weather.
Advance to meet slow or lob balls if opponents are not near
Do not allow a high lob to bounce in front of the goal.

Tipping

When tipping the ball over the cross-bar use two hands if possible with the palms under and the fingers on the near side of the ball. The ball is pushed up into the air, allowing its own momentum to carry it over the bar. This is used only as a last resort or when a shot from the field of play or a corner kick is likely to hit the cross-bar. When the ball is almost out of handling distance or is too fast to be handled by one hand, it should be tipped over the cross-bar or outside of the goal post.

Stress:

Give the ball plenty of clearance.
Use two hands if possible.
Get the hands on the near side of the ball.

Diving. (Note the right hand will hold the ball until the left hand can reach it.)

Diving

The body is flung toward the ball in a sideward dive with the lower hand reaching for the ball. The dive should be slightly forward rather than parallel to the goal line and not at right angles to the direction of the oncoming ball. This gives the ball an easier angle to clear the goal if it is to be pushed over the end-line as well as prevents the goalkeeper from crashing into the goal post. Sometimes a dive will bring the goalkeeper near enough to the ball so that he can scoop it under his body. In this case he should get two hands on it, start to get to his feet, look for the best direction in which to dodge, and be moving in that direction as he finally reaches his feet. When training goalkeepers to dive, use a sawdust pit until their fear of getting hurt is overcome.

Falling on the ball should not be confused with diving. To fall on the ball is poor playing, quite dangerous and should be done only in desperation. If the goalkeeper finds it necessary to fall on the ball, he should get to his feet quickly.

Stress:

Keep arms and hands away from the body.
Get to feet quickly.
Dive diagonally forward.
Hold onto the ball if possible.

Punching.

Punching

The ball is hit with either one or both clenched fists. The knuckles contact the ball. The wrists are in a straight line with the forearm, the power coming from the forward straightening of the arm.

Stress:

Punch the ball toward the sidelines.
Two fists are better than one.
The ball must not be missed.

Uses:

When there is no time to catch the ball.

To deflect a ball coming from the side as on a corner kick, a sharp angle short or a center.

When the ball cannot be reached to catch it because other players are in the way.

To deflect a ball too wet and heavy for the hand to tip over the cross-bar or around the goal post.

Striking.

Striking

The ball is hit with the side of the clenched fist and wrist. It should be hit with both arms if possible. The power comes from the forward swing of the arm or arms.

Stress:

Development of the weak arm.

Striking is safer than punching.

Eye *must* follow the ball and see it hit the arm.

Never use punching or striking unless the situation warrants their use.
Use very little force until skill is attained.

Uses:

 When there is no time to catch the ball.

 To return a ball coming from a forward direction.

 When near the goal line and there is danger of being charged into the goal if
 the ball is caught.

Dodging

*Dodging and bouncing. (Note the two hand
bounce will be a very low one.)*

Using the four steps allowed by the rules to evade the opponent's attempt at
charging is called dodging. If the opponent is coming in fast, move at right angles
to him; otherwise move diagonally in the direction from which he is coming and
pass to the side of him. A body feint may be used to help the dodge.

Bouncing (International)

The body bends forward to bring the hands close to the ground and the ball is
bounced only an inch or two. The head may be up with the eyes watching the field
of play. With opponents near, the less distance the ball has to travel from the time
it leaves the hand until it returns to the hand, the less chance there is for the
opponents to get the ball. Therefore, a two hand dribble is better than a one hand
bounce. With no opponents near, a goalkeeper may use a one hand waist high
dribble which will allow him to travel faster. It is better to bounce the ball every
third step rather than every fourth step as a measure of precaution against fouling.
Only the low bounce should be used on a wet or an uneven field, and then only in
case of emergency. Too much bouncing of the ball should be discouraged.

Stress:

 Advance the ball if possible before clearing.

 Carry the ball out to the side of the goal before getting rid of it.

 Do not start moving until the ball is securely held.

Clearing the Goal

Most beginners can throw with a greater degree of accuracy than they can punt or drop kick. The goalkeeper should, therefore, make this his first choice in clearing, being careful not to carry the ball back into the goal thus scoring for the opponents.

Throwing.—The throw that adapts itself best when there is plenty of time to clear is the baseball throw. The goalkeeper should learn to make the throw fast and low with either hand. The throw should be to a teammate, usually the inside forward, who should receive the ball on his sideline side. If time allows, a feint to throw in the opposite direction can well be used to draw the opponents away from the receiver. If hurried and there is no time to look for a teammate, the throw should be toward the opposite sideline from which the attack occurred.

Kicking.—When a *punt* is used to clear the goal, it should be kept low and toward the wing forwards. It is the second choice for clearing and should be used when there is no receiver open for a throw. A feint to punt may make an opening in the opponent's attack which will enable the goalkeeper to advance toward the penalty area line. This advance should give his teammates time to move into open places where they can receive a throw. If the goalkeeper's punts are too high, the foot is either meeting the ball too far in front of the body or too high in the air. It is very important that the goalkeeper learn to punt with either foot. A punt is made in the same manner as an instep volley kick.

Baseball Throw: (a) Arm and body in starting position; (b) Weight has shifted forward; (c) Follow through of arm and body.

Drop-kick.

A drop-kick is a better method of clearing when no opponents are near and there is no one to whom to throw the ball. It is much easier to keep low and accurate.

Goal Kicks

The instep kick or one of its variations is the best type to use provided the skill has been mastered. If a toe kick is ever to be allowed, it might be condoned on a goal kick taken with a dry ball and with the wind. The kick should be low and to the wings, preferably toward the wing opposite the side from which the ball is kicked. In no case should the ball be placed to the center of the field. A long kick is better than a pass to the backs except in unusual cases, such as kicking against a strong wind or kicking a wet, heavy ball. The goalkeeper should take these kicks, as the fullbacks get enough work in the course of the game without this added burden. One of the fullbacks should drop back and cover the goal while the kick is being taken.

Goal kick. (Note the fullback is in the goal while the goalkeeper takes the kick.)

CHAPTER VI

Analysis of Individual Positions

The players on a soccer team are called by the name which denotes their position at the start of and during the game.

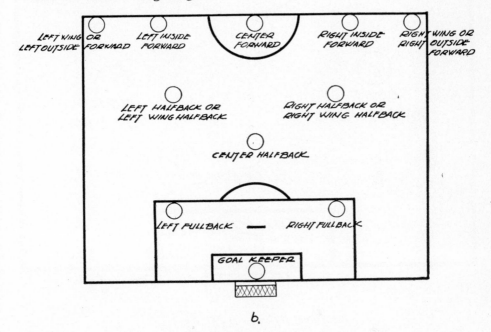

b.

Positions of players on an eleven-man team.

The duty of the forwards is to attack the opponent's goal, therefore, they rarely play defensively unless the ball is in offensive territory. The duty of the halfbacks is to back up the forwards in their attack on the opponent's goal and to help defend their own. This makes them half offensive and half defensive players. The duty of the fullbacks is entirely defensive in that their sole duty is to protect their own goal. The goalkeeper aids them in this by staying close to the goal at all times. To enable the goalkeeper to protect the goal better, he is allowed to use his hands on the ball. He may catch it, throw it, or kick it.

The players on an eight-man Soccer team are named in like manner. The team is formed by eliminating the center forward, the center halfback, and one of the fullbacks.

The only difference between the duties of the players on an eleven or eight-man team is that in the eight-man game the halfbacks play mostly defensive because of the short field, and the goalkeeper may play either offensive or defensive.

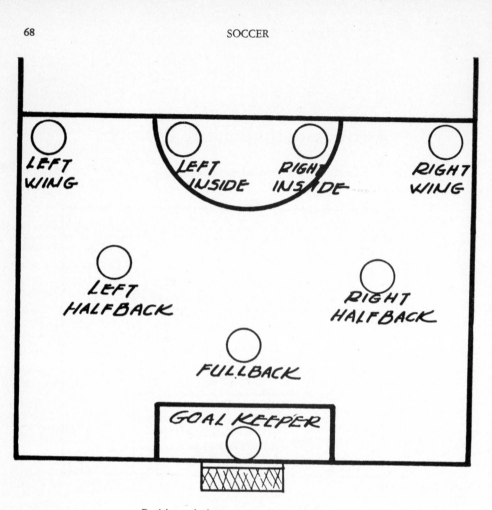

Positions of players on an eight-man team.

A quick method of selecting the first team for competition is to choose the *best players* and then to fill in the other positions with the *speediest runners*. If two players are of equal ability in handling the ball, then the faster one of the two, would be of more value in a game. Speed is never worth as much as skill but it is the next best substitute. A rough selection having been made on this basis, promotions or changes can be made as other players improve and earn a place on the next best team. The advantage of this method is that the players can immediately start to learn each other's style and to develop team play.

The duties of each player will vary according to the type of team offense and defense; therefore, no attempt has been made to make them too specific.

GOALKEEPER

A good basketball player will usually make a good goalkeeper because he is used to handling a fast ball with his hands and his left hand has probably already had some development. In cold weather the goalkeeper should be so dressed as to be warm, but the clothing must never be so heavy as to interfere with his efficiency. The goalkeeper must face the play while exercising to keep warm.

Position Play

On corner-kicks.—He should play near the far goal post, as this puts the entire play in front of him and it is easier to run forward than it is to run backward.

On penalty-kicks.—He plays mid-way between the goal post with his toes on the line, unless he has specific knowledge of the opposing team's penalty kicker that would require another position. He should be well balanced with his weight on his toes, his feet parallel and 18 to 24 inches apart. The parallel position of his feet will enable him to get a quicker start sideways by bringing into play the abductors of the foot as well as the extensors of the knee and ankle. If the ball is coming to his left, his first step should be with his left foot. As he takes the step, he should turn his body to that side so that he can launch his body at the ball along the goal line.

On shots from the field of play.—If a line were drawn from each goal post to the ball, the ball would have to travel within this angle in order to score. (This could be called the angle of possibility.) The goalkeeper should take a stance facing the ball and slightly toward the short side of the angle rather than directly in the center of it. The reason is that most shots are made toward the near goal post, and as the ball travels a shorter distance on this side of the angle, the goal tender has less time to play the ball. He should handle the ball about one yard out from the goal line.

When an opponent is dribbling the ball in alone.—If there is no chance of help from the goalkeeper's backs, the goalkeeper should advance at once for six or seven yards, to narrow the angle of possibility and decrease the dribbler's chance to score. The nearer the dribbler gets to the goal, the wider the angle of possible shot. When the dribbler is coming in with a teammate to whom he might pass, the goalkeeper should fake coming out and then either try to intercept the pass or drop back to normal position.

On opponent's free kicks.—He should direct the backs as to how far out they should play and tell them to move provided they are obstructing his vision.

On the defense.—He should talk to his backs and tell them if a man is not covered, if they are out of position, and if he intends to play the ball he should call out this intention in a loud voice. Having the entire field of play in front of him, he can direct the backs when and how hard to pass the ball back to him. In general, he should be the director of the defensive play.

There are only three times that a goal tender should leave his goal: (1) when he is positive that he can get the ball before an opponent; (2) on corner kicks when the ball is in the air and coming down in front of the goal; (3) in desperation to meet a dribbler, as mentioned above.

The goalkeeper should always use his hands. He should kick the ball only as a last resort when he could not possibly get his hands on it in time to save a score.

As most goalkeepers can throw with a much greater degree of accuracy than they can kick, they should throw rather than punt. A punt would be indicated only when all teammates within throwing range are covered.

The goal should be cleared to the side or side-diagonal and not to the center of the field. Balls cleared to the center, present the opponents with the best possible shot at the goal.

Skills to be Mastered

Catching
Throwing
Punting
Fisting
Deflecting ball around side of goal, or over the top
Two-hand dribble
Dodging while dribbling
Diving for ball
Falling on ball
Playing a slippery ball
Taking goal kicks
Defense against lone dribbler
Keeping in the angle of possibility
Proper stance and balance

FULLBACKS

Position Play

He should not crowd the goalkeeper or block his view.

— know how far out to play opponent's offside on free kicks.

— check the wing on penalty-kicks.

On corner kicks.—When the kick is taken on his side of the field, he should play about two yards out from the goal line and opposite the near goal post.

When the kick is taken on the opposite side of the field, he should play on the inside of the opponents' wing forward.

When own team is on offense

He should come out as far as safety will permit but rarely beyond the center of the field.

— not be on a line with his other fullback.

—attempt to slow up the opponent's attack to allow his halfbacks time to get back in their defensive position.

When own team is on the defense

He should cover his assigned man or his assigned zone.

— be quick to tackle.

— *never pass across in front of his own goal.*

— attack cautiously so as not to be beaten. When beaten by an opponent, he should immediately shift to the defensive position of his teammate who has gone out to cover the opponent.

—drop back into the goal when the goalkeeper moves out to handle the ball.

Skills to be Mastered

Goal kicks
Obstructing

Free-kicks
Tackling
Passing to goalkeeper
Long passes and kicks
Charging
Trapping
Heading
Dodging

HALFBACKS

The wing halfback, because his duties are both offensive and defensive, needs a great amount of endurance and courage to keep constantly hurrying the opponents. As he is in the best position to direct the play of the inside and wing forward on his side of the field he must be a good field general. A part of knowing where to direct the play is the ability to see the entire field of action in front of him; in other words, he must have field vision. As the halfback's shots are usually taken from at least sixteen yards out in the field of play, he must be able to make low power kicks.

Position Play

On offense

Backs up line on attack
Feeds ball to forwards
Shoots if it looks as if he had an opening for a shot
Sets ball up in front of goal

The halfback should be constantly looking for the opportunity to cross the ball to the opposite wing or to his own wing halfback. It is almost always good policy for the halfback to play the ball toward the opposite direction from which it came. The exception is when he is working a combination play with his own wing and inside. "Setting up the ball in front of the goal" is kicking the ball on a fly so that it will land about on the 6 yard line. It is used when the forwards are up near the goal and covered so that the success of a pass is doubtful.

On defense

Covers his own man or zone.
Gives directions to other backs.

On opponents' corner-kicks

Covers the opposing inside forward.
Plays between opponent and the goal.

On own corner-kicks

Backs up his line.
Sets up partial clearances of opponents or dribbles in or shoots.

On opponents' penalty kicks

Obstructs opposing inside.
Plays between his man and the goal or between his man and the kicker.

The play of the halfback after a penalty-kick is taken is not to rush toward the goal but to prevent the opponents' inside forward from following up the shot. This gives the goalkeeper a chance to recover the ball if he has fumbled or only partially stopped the shot.

On own penalty-kicks

Backs up line.
Is prepared to get back on the defense quickly.

On own team's kick-in

Usually takes the kick-in on his own side of the field.
Immediately after kick-in play gets into his normal position.

On opponents' kick-in

Performs assigned duty.
Looks to see where he will pass the ball if he gets possession of it.

On own free-kicks

Takes the kick if in his half of the field.
Covers his own man or zone after kicking.

On opponents' free-kicks

Covers the inside forward.
Plays opposing forwards' offsides.

Skills to be Mastered

Kick-in
Free-kick
Dribbling
Tackling
Charging
Calling for ball
Setting ball up
Feinting and dodging
Heading
Trapping
Passing

CENTER HALFBACK

Position Play

On offense

Backs up line.
Directs play of line and halfbacks.
Sets ball up in front of goal.
Shoots if opportunity presents itself.

On the defense

May cover opponents' center forward
Plays between center forward and goal.
Directs play of his own backs and line.

On opponents' penalty-kicks

  Covers opposing center forward.

  Plays between his man and the kicker

On own penalty-kicks

  May take the kick.

  If not, backs the play.

On opponents' corner-kicks

  Covers opposing center forward.

  Plays between his man and the goal.

On own free kicks

  May take kick in offensive half of field

  If not, backs play of line.

On opponents' free kicks

  Covers center forward.

  Helps pull opponents line off-side.

Skills to be Mastered

Same as for other halfbacks except throw-in.

SUGGESTIONS FOR ALL BACKS

There are times when backs should dribble, and other times when they should not. The back should not dribble when the ball is in his own penalty area, as the opponents are too likely to secure the ball in a favorable position to shoot. If it is necessary in order to get the kick away, the back may dodge an opponent, but that should be the extent of his dribbling in this dangerous territory. The halfback should not dribble in his own half of the field if one of his forwards is in position to receive a pass unless there is no opponent near him, and the opposing backs will retreat as he and his forwards advance. He should dribble in the offensive half of the field until he has drawn an opponent to himself when his forwards are all covered.

A back should not head the ball unless he has a good idea of where he is heading it. Usually fifty per cent of the balls headed go to the opponents. Heading by the backs is worthwhile if: (1) it is used as a pass to a teammate who is in the open; (2) it is in front of his own goal and the heading is to prevent the opponents from a scoring chance; (3) it is headed to a place where he can get it himself. Beginners cannot head a ball as far or control it as well as they can kick it with their feet.

Backs should constantly keep in mind that they are trying to prevent the opponents' forwards from getting the ball into a favorable position to shoot. With this in mind they should so tackle or place themselves as to prevent the forwards from dribbling the ball toward the center of the field. In other words, they should force the man with the ball toward the side lines and not allow him to cut inside of them toward the goal. In keeping with this idea of keeping the ball away from the center of the field, the backs will always attempt to clear the goal toward the side line, to take goal kicks toward the side lines, not to pass the ball across in front of the goal, and not to dribble in the penalty area.

The *ability to anticipate* the play of the opponents can be developed only by the back himself. When he learns this important ability, he will find that he not only improves as a player but also uses up much less energy. It can be developed by trying to see the opponents' attack as a whole and making mental notes of the system employed, and by "thinking smart." If the player will do this in every game, he will sooner or later develop the habit of anticipating the play of the opponents.

Whenever the goal is cleared, the backs should immediately move out from the goal. This causes the forwards to move out or become off-side and gives the goal-keeper a chance to see the ball. They should keep moving out and as far out as it is safe to do so. How far out it is safe to move depends upon the distance and accuracy of the kicks of the opponents' halfbacks and the relative speed of the opponents' forwards and the player's backs.

Backs should learn that *"one pass is worth two kicks,"* which is based upon the premise that a team must gain the distance of the field with the ball in their possession before they can get a chance to score. A pass is a sure gain of ground, while a kick is only a hope, with the odds being even as to whether their team or the opponents get the ball.

Jumping in the air to block a kick is one of the weaknesses of a beginning back and one of the most difficult habits to break in a player once it is established. The reasons for not jumping are: (1) it is a foul to jump at a player; (2) when off the feet the body is out of control, there is no chance for protection and injury is likely; (3) invariably when the player jumps, the ball will go under his feet.

On corner, penalty, and free-kicks near the goal the back best serves his team by obstructing his opponent's efforts to get to the ball. When the ball is coming toward him, he plays it, but if it is going to be played by the goalkeeper, he must give the goalkeeper a chance at the ball by delaying the opponents' attempt to converge on it. It is disconcerting enough to the goalkeeper to have all the attack rush at him, without having his own men add to this by also all rushing for the ball.

The situation sometimes arises when one of the fullbacks secures the ball and, hurried by the opponents in defensive territory, has no chance of passing to a team-mate, in which case it is sound strategy to kick the ball out of the field of play. This situation has given rise to such expressions as, "When in doubt, kick out," and "It is a wise back who knows his own side lines." It is also good defensive soccer to kick the ball over the side line when the defense is out of position or disorganized. While this gives the other team a kick in, it allows a team to organize its defense.

Fullbacks should attempt to slow up the attack so as to allow the halfbacks time to get back on the defense. When the forward with the ball is very deceptive and is likely to beat the back's attempt to tackle, the back can slow him up by retreating slowly while facing him from a distance of four or five feet. None of the forwards' tricks will work from this distance and the back is still near enough to tackle him if he should lose control of the ball momentarily.

When the backs are in position, they should not attempt to slow the attack by waiting tactics, but should immediately become aggressive. Now their object is to prevent the attack from getting set by hurrying the opponents. The sooner they stop the attack the better. It is best to stop the attack before it comes within shooting distance of the goal. Inexperienced backs have a tendency to race for the goal to defend it whenever the opponents launch an attack. This plays directly into the hands of the attack by allowing them to bring the ball easily up to within scoring distance.

In marking a clever forward the back should keep in mind that his chances to stop him are better if he can keep the ball from him or can keep him from getting control of the ball. Therefore, the back should mark him closely and be constantly "under his feet."

One of the fullbacks must cover the goal every time the goalkeeper leaves it to take goal-kicks, to go after corner kicks, or to advance with the ball.

The backs must decide in the case of all free kicks in defensive territory on how far out to play the opponents off-side. If they play too far out, a kick over their heads gives the forwards a chance to break through for a possible score. When they play too far back, a well-placed kick will still give the opponents a chance to score. A workable rule to help the backs make their decision is: play them just far enough off-side so that a kick over-head can be handled by the goalkeeper.

WINGS (OUTSIDE FORWARDS)

If the wing does not have a strong kick with each foot, but is one-footed, it depends largely on the style of offense which wing position he should play. When the attack calls for the wing to do much shooting, the right-footed player should play the left wing; when the attack calls for the wing to center the ball and shooting is incidental, the right-footed player should play the right wing.

The wing must have good judgment to make the correct decision as to whether to center, pass the ball, or to shoot. He should never be undecided and thus half center and half shoot, as this usually means that the ball misses the far goal post and goes over the goal line.

Position Play

On offense

Plays near side line.

Closes goal when deep in scoring territory.

Major duty is to carry ball deep into scoring territory and center.

If the wing plays close (one yard) to the side line, he is in a better position to receive a pass, because he spreads out the defense and fewer bad passes will go out of bounds since he has more time to get to the ball.

When the wing receives a pass, he should start the attack with all possible speed in order to "get the jump" on the defense. Fractions of seconds count and may make the difference between a successful attack or being "stopped cold" at midfield. Therefore wings should learn to use the deflection foot trap in order to receive a pass and start a dribble in one move. Only when closely covered by a back should the wing ever trap a pass or deflect the ball toward his own goal.

As the play nears the opponent's goal he should cut in so as to close that end and be in a position to shoot provided the ball comes through to him. He should get as near the goal as possible and still be on-side, so that if a shot at goal is taken, he can cut-in to prevent the shot from going wide of his goal post. He should attempt to center the ball low and hard, and should aim at the 6 yard line. A low hard center is quite likely to hit an opponent and go into the net. The goalkeeper has no chance to catch this type of center, especially if it is 6 yards out. A high center will be handled by the good goalkeeper even as far out as six yards.

On defense

Rarely goes into defensive half of field. Waits around center line for pass.

May mark opponent's wing on kick-in near midfield.

May go back to receive kick-in from own halfback or to meet a pass.

On own penalty-kicks

Usually plays just outside penalty area on the side.

Takes rebounds, and centers or shoots ball.

On own corner-kicks

Usually takes kick on his side.

Closes goal when kick is from other side.

If on a penalty kick the wing plays from the side of the penalty area and the fullback does not play nearer the goal, the wing is in an off-side position. He should start in when the kick is taken and continue in if the goalkeeper partially stops the ball; but if the ball hits the cross bar or goal post and rebounds, he should stop, turn his back on the play, and move back toward the side lines. Provided he does this, few referees will rule that he is interfering with the play or with an opponent.

When corner-kicks are taken from the far corner, he should be about 2 yards out from the goal line and on the goalkeeper's area line. His duty is to prevent the ball from coming through his territory, and whether he can best do this by closing in on the ball or holding his position must be left up to his judgment. In general, if he cannot get his head on the ball as it comes from the corner-kick, it is best for him to hold his position until he can see where the play will be next.

Skills to be Mastered

Dribbling

Feinting

Change of pace

Pivot-power-kicking

Passing

Shooting

Corner-kicking

Heading-down

The wing should learn to dribble the ball with the outside of his foot nearest to the side line. This has the advantage of keeping his body between an opponent and the ball, and will often cause an opponent to play the ball over the side line when he tackles.

On corner kicks the wing should aim at the 6 yard line as (1) few goalkeepers will come out this far because of the number of players in their way; (2) it allows the wing to miss his target by 6 yards and still keep the ball on the field. It is better to kick too far than to kick short of the center of the goal. The ball should come in fast and not too high, i.e., not lofted. The corner kick should be a pivot power-kick. Whether the ball curves away from or toward the goal is not as important as to be sure that it stays in the field of play. Allowance should be made for the wind. When it is blowing strongly toward the goal, it is safer to kick a ball that will curve against the wind.

INSIDE FORWARDS

Position Play

On offense

Plays between and slightly back of wing and center forward.
Sets up plays.
Is careful not to be so far forward that ball is centered behind him.

As the most important duty of the inside forward is to set up plays, he should always attempt to think one move in advance. In other words, he should be constantly asking himself what he should do when the ball comes to him. This calls for always knowing the positions of the other players. Once a player develops this habit, he will not have to stop to think what to do with the ball after he gets it and will not thus give the defense a chance to get set.

Nothing is more annoying to a wing than to see a perfectly centered ball go behind his inside forwards and out to the other side of the field, as happens when the inside forwards in their eagerness to get near the goal, move up even with the center forward and into the goal area. It is better for the insides to be back too far than in too close, for they can always move in by a burst of speed and are then in position to shoot.

On defense

May cover opponents' wing halfback.
Must be ready for fast break offensively.

On own corner kicks

On a kick from the far corner plays opposite goal post; on a kick from the near corner plays 2 yards toward center of goal, 6 to 8 yards out from goal line.
Heads ball down into goal whenever possible.

On opponent's corner kicks

May cover opponent's wing halfback.
Starts attack by passing to wing or center forward.

On own penalty kick

Plays near kicker.
Follows in quickly for rebound.

On opponent's penalty kick

May cover opponent's wing halfback.
Plays between his man and the kicker.

Skills to be Mastered

Passing
Dribbling
Heading
Shooting
Trapping
Feinting
Tackling

CENTER FORWARD

Position Play

On offense

Leads the attack and sets up plays.
Plays center of offensive half of field from center line to goal.
Plays even with wings when attack starts.
Receives "centers" from wings, and shoots for goal.

When his team is on the defense he stations himself just on-side and is ready (1) to go to an open place to receive a pass from his own players, or (2) to prevent the opponent's fullbacks from getting a loose ball and setting it up.

On defense

Usually has no defensive duties except to cover any loose balls around midfield.
May cover opponent's center half when half is dribbling ball up field.

On own penalty kicks

May take the kick.
When he doesn't take kick, plays as close to kicker as possible, ready to go in for rebounds.

On own corner kicks

Plays in front of goal, on 6 yard line, ready to play kick for goal.
May screen or obstruct goalkeeper.

If the center forward is to screen or obstruct the goalkeeper on corner-kicks, when the kick is taken he must go toward the place where the ball is going to land, so as to be "on-side" when it is played.

Skills to be Mastered

Shooting
Trapping
Passing
Dribbling
Heading
Penalty kicking
Pivoting and feinting
Tackling

SUGGESTIONS FOR ALL FORWARDS

To score is the ultimate object of all forwards. When the forwards outnumber the opponent's backs, the attack should be pressed with all possible speed. In other words the forwards, even the wings, should not hesitate to leave their normal position when by so doing they can speed up the attack.

If a wing has a chance to dribble the ball toward the goal, he should do so, rather than toward the corner flag. This will cut down the length of his centering kick to a pass and will permit greater accuracy.

A forward should not try to dribble past two backs in succession. When he has only one back to beat, he is justified in trying to do so alone, provided he will then be in a favorable position to shoot for the goal.

Forwards should know and constantly practice feints. The use of a pivot or feint will often gain for the forward that step or fraction of a second that is necessary in order for him to get a pass or a shot away, and often makes the difference between keeping or losing possession of the ball. It disturbs the opponents and makes them more cautious. Inexperienced players often try to kick the ball through an opponent. The impossibility of this must be brought to their attention, and they must be taught to pass around or pull the ball to the side of the opponent before kicking.

When the ball is in the air in front of the goal, forwards should attempt to head it down whether shooting for the goal or not. When the ball is on the ground in front of the net the goalkeeper's vision of it is at least partially obscured. If it is in the air, the goalkeeper always has the chance to get his hands on it, and he can see it plainly. The chances of scoring a goal are better when the ball is headed down, since it takes the goalkeeper a fraction of a second longer to field a low ball.

A shot from near the goal is an attempt to pass the ball by the goalkeeper and not to kick it through him. Power is not nearly so important as accuracy. It may be more fun to blast the ball into the net, but this tendency has caused many players to miss certain goals.

Many goals from close in are missed because players hesitate on chest-high balls, trying to decide whether to use their foot or their head on the ball when neither should be used. The ball should be played off the chest into the goal. It is well to remember that the ball can be trapped, as well as kicked, into the goal.

When the ball is in front of the goal and within scoring range, it should not be passed out to the wing. When the forwards are all closely covered, and there seems no chance for a shot, a pass back to the halfback is indicated. He can keep the ball in the center and either dribble in and pass or shoot. If it is the halfback's intention to shoot, the forwards should help him by drawing the opponents away from the mouth of the goal.

Forwards must keep positioning themselves so as to receive a pass. When marked they should attempt to either get away from their marker into an open space or play between their marker and the ball. When they are not marked they should get in an open space. Always come to meet the pass, if opponents are near or the pass is slow.

Forward lines are as good as their teamwork.—Poor forwards working together are often better than good forwards working alone. The forwards, with the backs, should give directions to each other. The attack will be as good as the directions given and accepted. The forward with the ball should not be forced to accept full responsibility for it. He should be informed by his teammates when a player is approaching from behind, when and where to pass, when to dribble or try a trick, or when to shoot. The other part to the giving of directions, if good teamwork is to be obtained, is the acting upon them. Together these tend toward good team play, alone they do not.

In general, it is the wing's duty to advance the ball, and close the goal, the inside's duty to help in the advancement and to shoot, and the center forward's to set up plays and shoot. However, when the opponent's backs gain possession of the ball in the offensive half of the field the forwards should make every effort to take it away from or to hurry them.

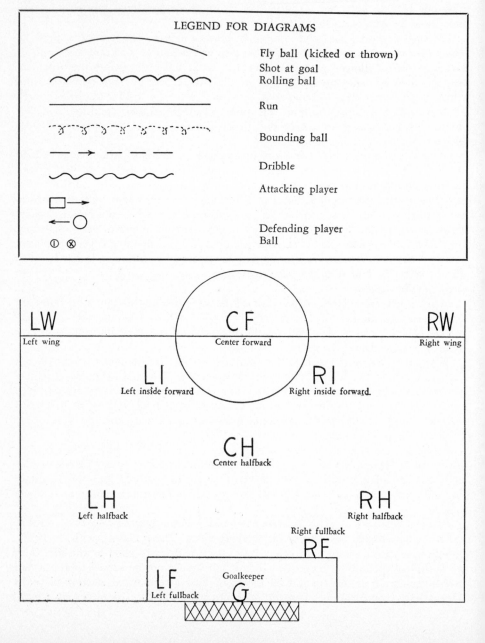

LEGEND FOR DIAGRAMS

Fly ball (kicked or thrown)
Shot at goal
Rolling ball

Run

Bounding ball

Dribble

Attacking player

Defending player
Ball

LW — Left wing
CF — Center forward
RW — Right wing
LI — Left inside forward
RI — Right inside forward
CH — Center halfback
LH — Left halfback
RH — Right halfback
RF — Right fullback
LF — Left fullback
G — Goalkeeper

CHAPTER VII

Game Situations

As ball control is the summation of all the skills of manipulating the ball, so the game itself is the summation of all the plays or situations occurring in it.

The International rules have been modified by the National Collegiate Athletic Association in several respects. Namely: the goal keeper may not be charged at any time and is allowed only four steps to clear the ball; the sliding tackle is illegal; the penalty area is an eighteen-yard arc (see diagram on page 83); the ball is kicked-in rather than thrown-in from the side lines.

The kick-in plays and zones of both offense and defense are equally suited to the throw-in plays called for by the International Rules under which the Olympic Games are played.

Starting a Game

Before the start of a game the captains of the teams playing meet at the center of the field to toss a coin. The winner of the toss has the option of choosing which goal he will defend or the kick-off. If he choose the goal, the opposing team kicks off. If he choose the kick-off, the opposing team has the choice of which goal they will defend. The game is started by a kick-off from the center of the field. The ball is kicked off when it has turned over once in a forward direction. On the kick-off all players must be in their own half of the field and no opponents may be nearer than 10 yards to the ball. As soon as the kick is taken, players may move into the opponents' half of the field. The teams then alternate in kicking-off to start the three ensuing periods of the game. In case of a score, the team scored against re-starts the game by a kick-off. Kick-off plays are designed to retain possession of the ball and to advance it toward the opponents' goal.

Kick-Off

Offense.—The center forward kicks off to the right inside, who passes to the

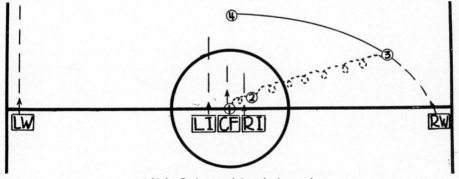

A kick-off play involving the forwards.

right wing. The right wing dribbles in until he draws a back and then crosses the ball to the other side of the field or to the center forward. The right inside might pass to the left wing or straight ahead to the center forward. As soon as the ball is touched by the center forward, all forwards except the inside that the ball is passed to sprint down the field.

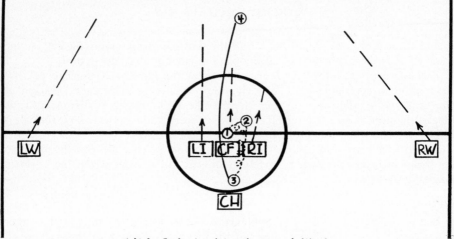

A kick-off play involving the center halfback.

The center forward passes to the right inside, who passes back to the center halfback. The center half makes a long kick down the field. The wing forwards cut in to help the left inside and center forward receive the ball. The success of the play hinges on getting four forwards and the ball down the field in territory guarded only by the fullbacks.

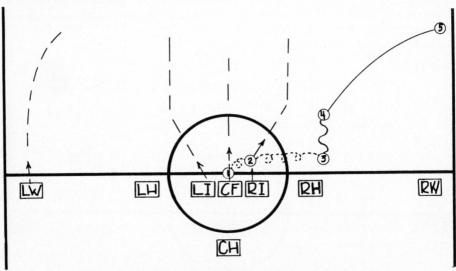

A kick-off play involving the wing halfback.

The center forward passes to the right inside, who passes to the right halfback He dribbles forward until a back is drawn to him and then passes to the right wing, who centers.

The right inside might pass the ball back to the center half, who would then have the choice of passing to either wing halfback, the same play continuing from that pass.

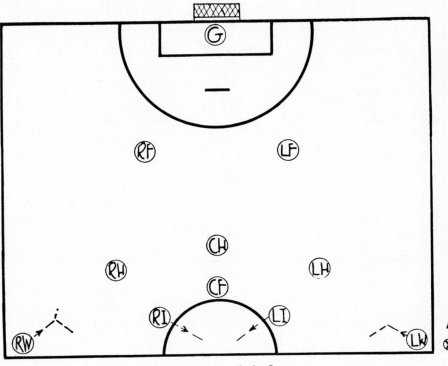

Defense on kick-off.

Defense.—The inside forwards rush in to break up the play or to hurry the opponents so that they may make a bad pass. When the ball is passed back to the center halfback, the inside forwards follow the ball back to block the kick. The center forward holds his position to break up any play through the center, and the wing forwards drop back slightly to cover the opponents' wing forwards and prevent their receiving a pass. The halfbacks mark the center and the inside forwards as they come through the forward line. The fullbacks hold their position until the play becomes apparent and then move to mark their men or to cover their territory. In case of a long kick up the center the fullbacks can pass to the goalkeeper and let him clear the ball.

Variation.—The center forward moves in one or two steps and then stops to break up any play through the center. The left inside comes in fast from the center line to hurry the play if the kick-off is made to the opponent's right inside. The right inside does the same to the opponent's left inside, but his approach is more

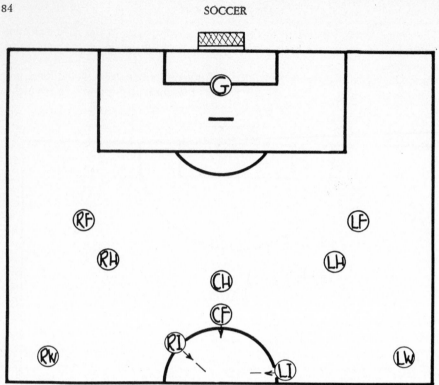

Variation of kick-off defense.

from the front. The wing halfbacks cover the space between the center and inside forwards. The center-half backs up the center forward. The wing forwards cover the opponent's wing forwards by lining up ten yards away from the center line, and preventing the opponent's wings from cutting in for a pass.

Kick-in

When the whole of the ball passes over the side line, either on the ground or in the air, it is out of play. The ball is put into play at the point it left the field by the team opposite from the one that last touched it before it went out by means of a kick-in. At the moment of kicking the ball into play, the ball must be on or outside the side line, it must be motionless, and the kicker must be off the field of play. The ball may be kicked in any direction. The player making the kick-in may not play it again until it has been touched or played by another contestant. A goal may not be scored directly from the kick-in.

This situation is an important one to practice, both because it occurs frequently in a game and because it is an important ground gainer and may lead to a scoring chance. As the type and object of kick-in will depend largely on the place from which the ball is to be kicked, and as the defense is somewhat dependent upon this, for discussion, the field will be divided into three sections.

Signals should be used to indicate the kick-in play. The players taking the kicks in the defensive and offensive parts of the field must be careful not to make

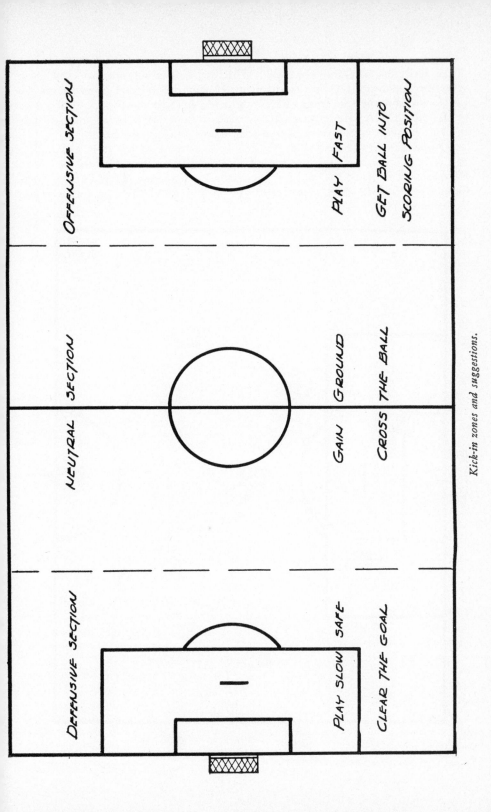

Kick-in zones and suggestions.

illegal kicks, as these are very costly. When the ball is improperly kicked in, it gives the opponents a chance to cover up. Usually it is a good play to cross the ball to the opposite side from which it is kicked in. Kicks to the wing should be to his feet; to the inside forward, feet or head; to the center forward and halfback, the feet or head; to the fullback, the feet; to the goalkeeper, chest high.

Offense (Defensive Section of Field).—The purpose of the team kicking the ball in is to move the ball from defensive to offensive territory. To lose the ball to the opponent is dangerous, and for this reason the play used should be a safe one. Caution is needed, which means that the kick-in should be taken slowly and deliberately.

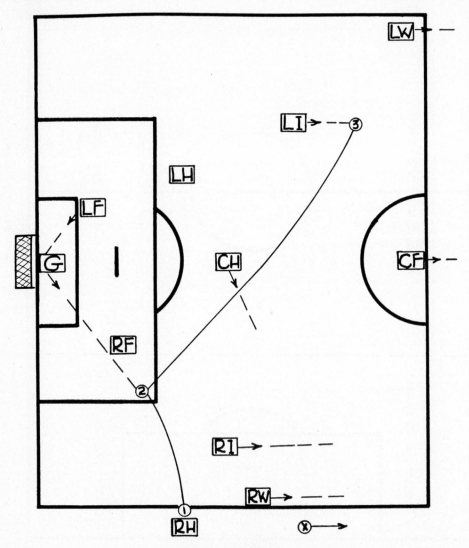

Kick-in to goalkeeper.

A kick to the goalkeeper is the safest and the greatest ground gainer and should be given first choice. The success of the play depends upon the ability of the forwards and the center half to decoy the opponents away from the penalty area. The right half taking the kick should feint a kick to the wing before kicking to the goalkeeper. The goalkeeper punts or throws the ball to the opposite side of the field. One fullback comes in to cover the goal and the other backs up the goalkeeper. If one of the opponents comes in to cover the goalkeeper, the kick might be made to the man thus left unmarked. The next safest play is a long kick to the wing or inside forward, thus keeping the ball away from the center of the field.

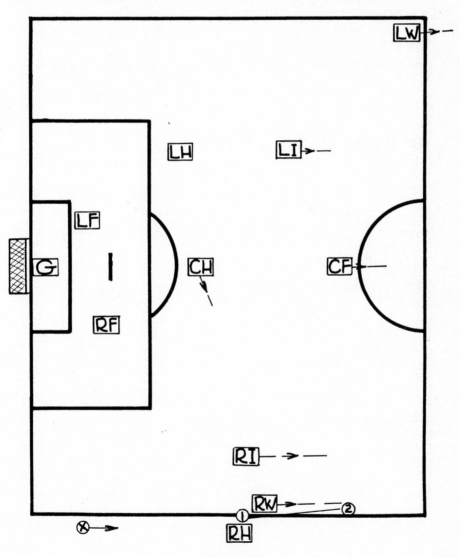

Kick-in to wing.

Variation.—The kick is made to the feet of the wing and between the wing and the side line. A kick to the inside may be made to either the head or the feet. If the kick is to the wing and he beats his opponent, he may continue down the side lines; otherwise, he should cross-pass to the center or opposite forwards. The inside forward, usually in a crowd of players, upon receiving the ball should immediately cross it or pass it to his own wing forward.

A kick to the center forward or halfback is dangerous and therefore seldom used.

Defense (Defensive Section of Field).—A man-for-man defense is the advisable type, as the kicks are made to individuals and zones are too numerous to cover adequately. The defensive players should attempt to keep one step ahead of and on the inside of the men they are marking.

As the forwards are always available in this territory, they should be used to mark the opponent's forwards closely.

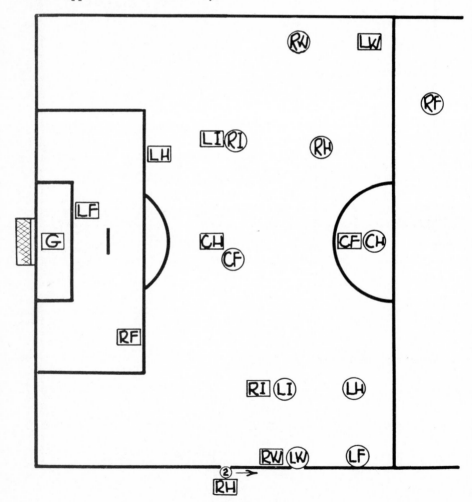

Kick-in defense using forwards.

The exceptions are that the center forward marks the opponent's center half, and the wing on the opposite side of the field gets in the clear to receive a pass. The left half and the fullback act as a secondary line of defense and are in position to handle any extra long kicks. The wing on the side of the kick marks his man closely but leaves him and covers the player making the kick as soon as it is evident that the ball is not coming to his man. If the goalkeeper leaves his goal, the inside forward goes in to mark him and the left half covers the opponent's inside forward. The fullback on the opposite side of the field places himself to intercept any cross field pass.

Offense (Neutral Section of Field).—The purpose here is to gain ground and to retain possession of the ball. As this territory is not dangerous, more players can be called into the play, making a greater variety of plays possible. Passes should be of the shorter rather than the longer type and should be taken promptly.

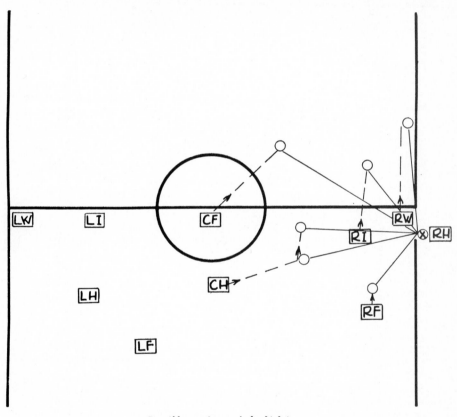

Possible receivers of the kick-in.

A kick may be made to the wing as in the diagram on page 87 or it may be made to the center or inside forwards. It may be made to the center half, who either passes up to the center forward, crosses to the opposite wing or inside, dribbles up field, or passes back to the right half. When opponents are all decoyed away from the fullback, the kick could go to him, in which case, the center half should start toward the ball but veer away so as not to block the fullback's reception of the pass.

If the kick is to the forwards, they should work the ball up the field by short passing unless the defense has left the opposite wing forward open for a long pass to the corner. In case the kick is to the backs, they should start a dribble until an opening for a pass appears.

Defense (Neutral Section of Field).—When the kick is to be taken from around midfield, the forwards can be used to mark the opponent's forwards as in the diagram below. If the kick-in is too far back of the midfield line and the wing is used to mark the wing, it weakens your offensive strength. In this case the wing could mark the one making the kick to prevent his getting a return pass and also could hustle the fullback should the kick be made to him. See diagram below. The left half is ready to play a long kick or to back up the fullback and inside

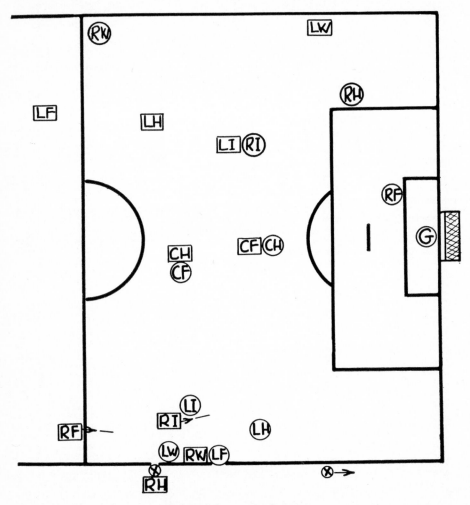

Kick-in defense neutral section.

forward. The right fullback moves over to mark any opponent breaking through, while the right half guards against cross passes to the far corner.

Offense (Offensive Section of Field).—The object in this territory is to get the ball into scoring position. Therefore the ball must be put into play quickly and before the defense can get into position to defend against the kick. In order to accomplish this the kick is often made by the wing forward or in some cases by the inside forward. The kick is made to any player open to receive it, preferably the inside and center forward. When the defense is set before the ball can be recovered for the kick, then a return pass to the kicker is probably the best play.

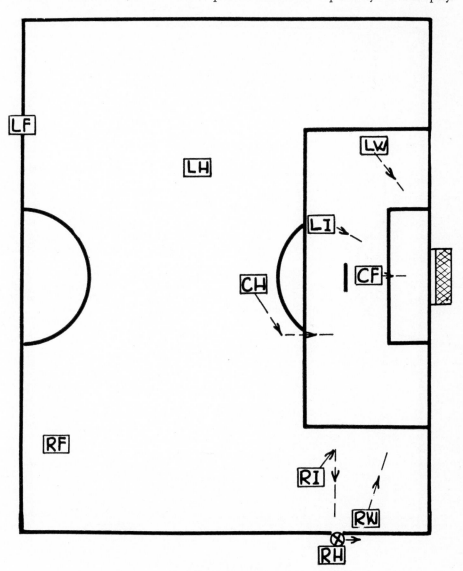

Pass back to kicker.

The ball is kicked to the inside forward, who starts toward the goal and then cuts back toward the side line. He receives the ball on his chest and plays it back to the kicker, who sets the ball up to the far side of the goal or dribbles toward the corner and centers. The wing must decoy his marker away from the play by calling for the ball and running toward the goal. The center half moves toward the kick and then up into the place vacated by the inside forward. Alternate plays from this setup are kicks to the wing, center forward, center halfback, or to a clear place near the mouth of the goal.

Defense (Offensive Section of Field).—When the defending team is ahead,

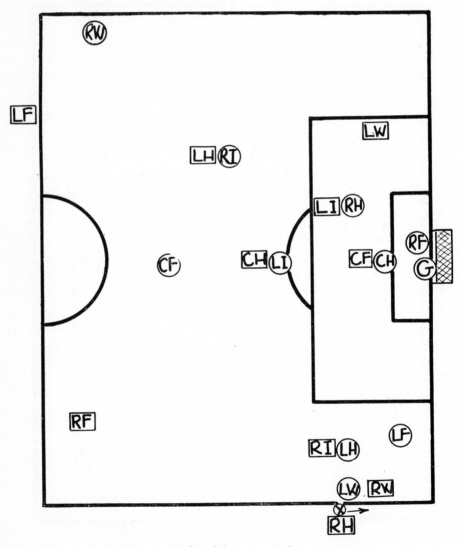

Kick-in defense near goal.

they can afford to weaken their offense for the moment by using the forwards to strengthen the defense.

The left wing would mark the kicker and the opponent's wing as long as that player is near the kicker. If the opponent's wing cuts for the goal he is marked by the left fullback, who is also blocking any kick to a clear spot in front of the goal. The right fullback moves over to the front of the goal to mark any opponent breaking through the defense, and at the same time is ready to cover the far-side wing if the ball should be crossed. The center forward and right wing move back to open places to be in position to receive clearing passes.

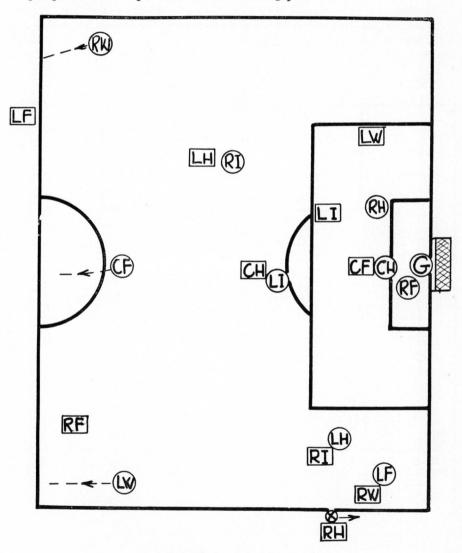

Variation of kick-in defense near goal.

When the defending team is on the short end of the score, the left wing should play toward the center of the field and the opponent's wing should be marked by the left fullback. This leaves the offense relatively strong and ready to start a three-man fast break for the opponent's goal.

Goal Kick

When the whole of the ball passes over the goal line, excluding that portion between the goal posts, either in the air or on the ground, having last been played by one of the attacking team, it shall be kicked forward directly into play beyond the penalty-area, from a point within that half of the goal-area nearest to where it crossed the line, by a player of the defending team. The ball is not in play until it has come out of the penalty area. When the goal kick fails to come out of the penalty area or is played before it comes out of the penalty area, the kick is retaken.

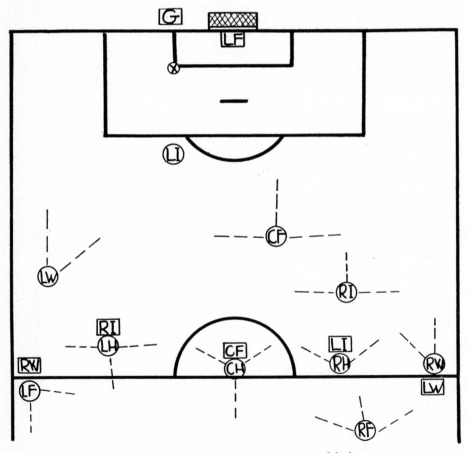

Lop-sided "V" formation on opponent's goal kick.

From opponent's goal.—The backs each mark a forward wherever the forward may be and play nearer their own goal in case of a long kick.

The inside forward on the side from which the kick is being taken plays just outside the penalty area and in front of the ball. The other forwards play in the shape of a lop-sided "V" with the inside being the point of the "V." The areas they are to cover are shown by dotted lines.

The fullback on the opposite side of the field from the kick drops back and is ready to mark the wing or the center forward if they break through with the ball.

This formation works well against a team that crosses their goal kicks and is an easy one from which to start an attack. It is a modification of the straight "V" diagrammed below.

"V" formation on opponent's goal kick.

From own goal.—The goalkeeper takes the kick.

One fullback covers the goal until relieved by the goalkeeper and then moves to his defensive position. The other fullback marks the opponent's center forward.

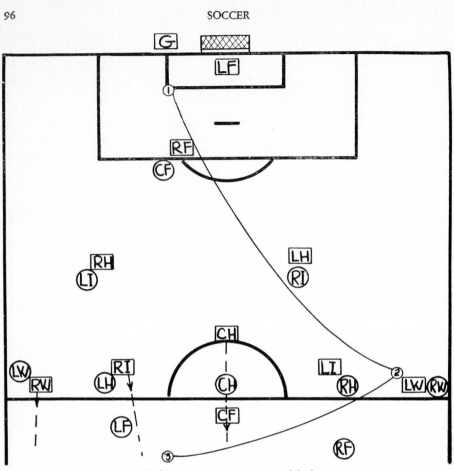

Marking opponents on own goal kick.

The wing halfbacks cover the opponent's inside forwards. The center half, in the middle of the field, starts to the side that the ball is to travel with the run of the goalkeeper. The goalkeeper indicates the side he will kick to by a prearranged signal. The forwards on that side play near enough to the goal so that the kick would travel over their heads if they did not move out with the kick. The object of this is to take the ball on the head if possible but in any case to be moving in the direction of the ball. Upon receiving the ball, they should cross-field pass toward the opponent's goal. The wing and inside forward on the opposite side from which the ball is to be kicked move up the field with the goalkeeper's run to be able to handle a cross-field pass and with the center forward launch a quick attack. They must guard against getting off-side.

Off-Side

A player is off-side when ahead of the ball in the opponent's half of the field and there are not two opponents nearer their own goal-line *when the ball is last played* unless he or an opponent last played it. A player cannot be off-side on a goal kick, corner kick, throw-in or drop ball until the ball has been again played. A player is not penalized for being in an off-side position unless in the opinion of the referee he is interfering with the play or an opponent, or is seeking to gain an advantage by being off-side. When a player is off-side, he can only be put on-side by an opponent playing the ball, by being behind the ball when it is played, or if ahead of the ball, by having two opponents between him and their own goal line when the ball is played.

Corner Kick

When the whole of the ball passes over the goal line, excluding that portion between the goal posts, either in the air or on the ground, having last been played by one of the defending team, a member of the attacking team shall take a kick from within the quarter-circle at the nearest corner flag-post, which must not be removed. A goal may be scored direct from such a kick.

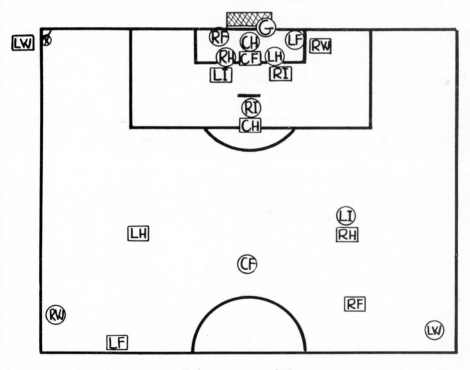

Defense on corner kick.

Defense.—The goalkeeper plays at the far goal post and is ready to play any fly ball in the goal area.

The backs each mark an opponent and obstruct him from playing the ball. The fullback on the side from which the kick is taken plays opposite the goal posts to prevent a low ball crossing the mouth of the goal.

The back nearest the landing point of the ball attempts to play the ball unless the goalkeeper signifies his intention to do so.

The right inside marks the center half but is ready to cover the left wing half in case of a clearance to that side. The center forward drops back halfway between the center and penalty area lines to cover any loose balls in the center of the field. The wing forwards drop back to a clear spot to be ready to receive any clearing passes, all of which should be made to them.

If the ball is going to land outside the goal area, all the backs should at once move out and attempt to carry the ball up the field and to the wing forwards. This forces the opponents to leave the vicinity of the goal or be placed in an off-side position and gives the goalkeeper a clear view of the ball.

Each member of the team should be trained to judge the direction and force of a kick as soon as it leaves the kicker's foot, the same as baseball outfielders are trained to judge the flight of a baseball as it leaves the bat.

Offense.—The attack used to demonstrate the defense against the opponent's corner kick is one that is commonly used. A variation that might be used would be to move up both wing halfbacks and drop the center half back to mark the center forward. In this case the fullbacks can mark the wing forwards and make the opponent's attack more difficult to get started.

The right wing closes the far end of the goal area to center the ball in case the kick is too long. If the goalkeeper goes out to deflect the ball, the wing should

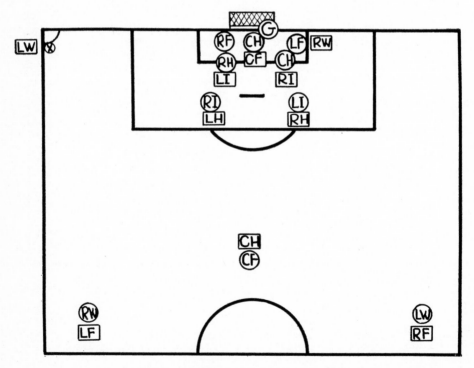

Positions of offensive players on corner-kick.

anticipate the direction in which the ball will be deflected and start moving back to intercept and center it. When the ball is not coming to the wing and the goalkeeper is not making a play on the ball, it is best for the wing to hold his position, move to remain on-side, and be ready to go in on the goal if the ball starts his way.

The center and inside forwards should move in on the ball and attempt to head it either *down* into the net or *down* in front of the goal. They should try to so position themselves that they are moving in on the ball rather than moving back for it. They might try to cause their markers to be out of position by staying out of position until the moment before the kick is taken and then moving in.

The wing halfbacks hold their positions when the ball is in front of the forwards and are ready to retrieve any short clearances. If the ball is just in back of the forwards, a pass back to the halves for a shot by them is the best play. In which case the forwards should move away from the mouth of the goal and by calling for the ball try to draw their markers with them to give the halfback an opening for his shot.

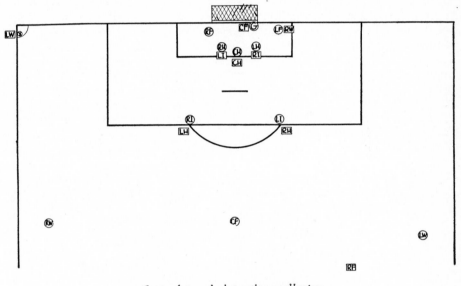

Center forward obstructing goalkeeper.

Variation.—A variation is to use the center forward to obstruct the goalkeeper.

The center forward takes a wide stride stance in front of and close to the goalkeeper, facing the ball. His duty is to obstruct the view of the goalkeeper as the kick is made and to impede the goalkeeper's progress toward the ball by going slowly toward its landing place. When properly executed, one of the teammates of the center forward should have an opportunity to play the ball before the goalkeeper can reach it. The center forward must make sure that he is on-side at the time the ball is played in front of the net. The center half moves up to fill in the place vacated by the center forward, and the wing halfbacks drop back to the penalty area line.

The accuracy of the corner kickers plus the score and time left to play are the determining factors in deciding which type of attack to use. The attack in the diagram on page 97 is neither weak offensively nor defensively and is possibly the best to use with inaccurate kickers. The attack diagrammed on page 98 is stronger offensively and defensively than that on page 97 but calls for more accuracy on the part of the kicker. The attack shown on page 99 is strong offensively, weak defensively, and calls for accurate corner kicking. When a team is behind, it should use the attack on page 99 to make the best possible use of the corner kick advantage, but if ahead, either that on page 97 or 98 would be indicated. This, however, must be left to the judgment of the captain, who should indicate by signal which formation is to be used. A team would be justified in throwing all the halves and fullbacks into the formation in a last minute effort to score, when by so doing they could tie or win the game.

Drop Ball

When the ball is kicked out of the playing field and the referee cannot determine which team last played it, or when the game has been temporarily suspended, the ball is put in play by being dropped between two opposing players. The ball is dropped from waist height by the referee and is in play when it touches the ground. If the ball is played before it touches the ground, it is not in play and should be dropped again.

The drop ball could not be classed as an important situation on the basis of how many times it occurs in a game, but when it occurs in front of or near the goal, its importance is magnified. Therefore it should be practiced to familiarize the players with their duties.

In front of own goal.—The goalkeeper should be on the goal line. The backs should play between opponents and the goal and check closely man-for-man. The player taking part in the "drop" may use the sole of foot or the two foot tackle for his initial movement and then clear provided he has succeeded in holding the

Drop ball. (Showing the defensive player using a one-foot tackle to hold the ball.)

ball. If he tries a kick for his initial movement, the ball may pass under him or bounce off his opponent into the goal. His stance should be in the center of the angle of possible shot and as near the ball as the referee will allow, as his chief duty is to block a direct kick to the goal. To disguise his real intention he should make it appear to his opponent that he is going to kick hard at the ball.

In front of opponent's goal.—The forwards should attempt to take as first choice an uncovered position, as second choice a position nearer the ball than their marker, or if closely marked, as a third choice a position farther away from the goal than the drop to draw their marker out and leave a clear space in front of the goal. The player taking the "drop" should attempt to pass the ball over in front of the goal but outside of the goalkeeper's reach, or to score direct.

PENALTIES

When a foul has been committed, the penalty is a free kick or a penalty kick awarded to the opponents at the point where the violation was made. Free kicks are divided into two groups, those from which a goal may be scored by kicking the ball directly into the goal (called direct free kicks), and those which must be played or touched by some other player after the kick is taken before they may result in a score (indirect free kicks). Indirect free kicks are awarded for minor infractions of rules, such as goalkeeper taking more than four steps with the ball,

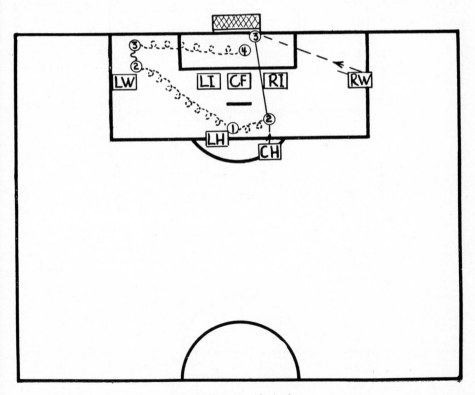

Two indirect free kick plays.

dangerous play, illegal substitution, off-side, or playing the ball before another player touches it after throwing it in or taking a free kick.

Indirect Free Kick

A situation that is similar to and is played like the direct free kick unless it is taken from within or close to the penalty area. When the kick is allowed close to the goal, the offense and defense have various tactics which they might employ, each governed to some extent by the tactics employed by the other. The play to be used should be called by the kicker and not indicated by his looking at the man who is to receive the pass. The success of the play depends upon the timing of the pass and the shot at the goal.

Attack.—The diagram shows the left halfback taking a short kick. He may pass the ball to the center half, who shoots, or he may pass to the left wing, who dribbles toward the goal line and centers the ball in back of the defense. The right wing should play wide to draw out a defensive player. If he does not succeed in so doing, he should move in to try to close the goal on that side.

Variations.—The left halfback pivot kicks with the left foot to the right wing coming in for a shot.

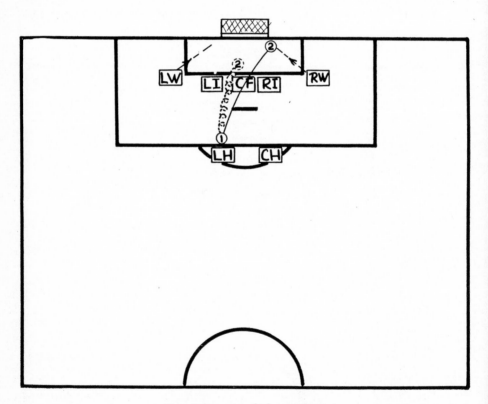

Two indirect free-kick variations.

Provided the left inside and the center forward can so maneuver that they are standing side by side with no opponent between them, a fast pass into this opening will allow for an easy scoring chance.

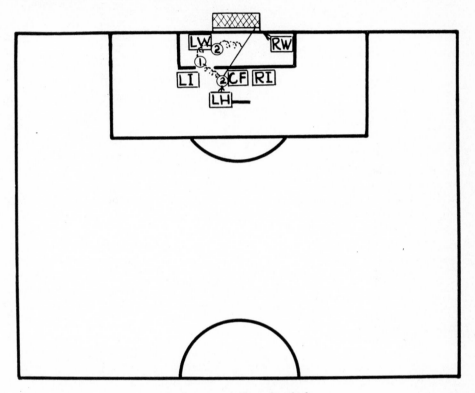

Back pass on indirect free kick.

Variation.—When the kick is allowed within ten yards of the goal, it is often best to take it in a backward direction or the defense will be on the ball in time to prevent a good scoring chance. Two possibilities are shown in the above diagram. The pass to the left half is probably the best play, as he will have more time to get his kick off. His shot at the net near the far goal post, if missed, might be played by the right wing, which would give it the preference over the near post. The alternate play of passing to the left wing and then to the center must be well disguised by feinting in the opposite direction to have a chance for success.

Defense.—The backs should each mark a man, and play on the inside of him. The left fullback does not mark the right wing closely but is ready to intercept any pass made to him or to mark or obstruct him if he comes in to make a play. The inside forwards come back into the defense and as soon as the kick is taken move out to cover the halfbacks. The goalkeeper plays slightly to the short side of the angle of possible shot and one yard out from the goal line. He should have an unobstructed view of the ball and should be aided in this by the backs. The backs should play the opponents as far off-side as possible, which is within ten **yards of the ball.**

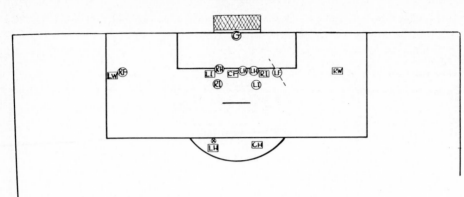

Defense on indirect free kick near penalty area.

Variation.—In the case of an indirect free kick within ten yards of the goal, the rules allow the defense to be nearer than ten yards to the ball with the provision that they stand on the goal line and between the goal posts. One plan of defense is to bring all players back and, with the goalkeeper standing in the angle, alternate the backs and forwards on the goal line. As the kick is taken, the forwards rush forward to smother the kick and attempt to carry the ball with them up the field. The backs hesitate a moment to protect the goal and then move out to mark the opponent's forwards. The goalkeeper might take one step forward or backward with the kick to obtain more freedom for sideward movement.

Direct Free Kicks

They are awarded for serious infractions of rules such as tripping, kicking, striking, jumping at an opponent, handling the ball, holding, pushing, violent charging, charging from behind, or charging an opponent when he has two feet off the ground.

Offensive tactics.—A free kick provides a scoring opportunity when allowed in the offensive half of the field. The nearer the penalty area the kick is awarded the

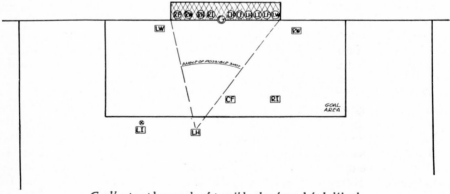

Goalkeeper plays angle of possible shot from left halfback.

more dangerous it becomes for the defensive team. Any mistakes of the defense should be capitalized on by the attack.

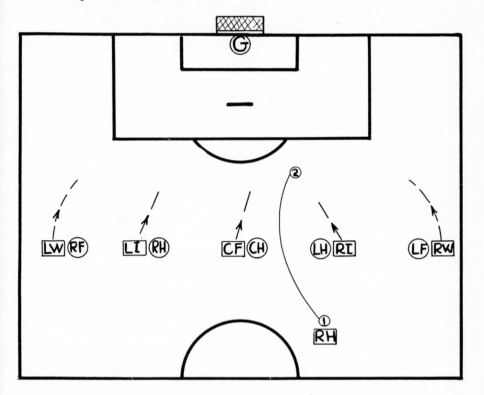

Backs playing too far from goal.

When the defense plays too far out from the goal, a kick over the heads of the players is indicated, followed by a rush toward the goal by the forwards as the kicker's foot meets the ball.

When the backs play too near the goal, the ball may be either set up in front of the goal, or passed to a teammate for a shot. The forwards attempt to block the goalkeeper's view of the ball.

A free kick awarded near the penalty area can be used for a shot at the goal if the team has a strong accurate kicker. The plays as outlined for an indirect free kick can also be used in this situation. When the free kick is to be taken from the side of the penalty area, a hard cross-pass to the opposite wing cutting in fast for the goal is a good play. The opposite inside forward should also advance toward the goal in case the kick is low or short.

Defensive tactics.—The opponents should be played far enough off-side so that a ball kicked over the heads of the defensive backs may be played by the goalkeeper before the opponents can reach it. The goalkeeper's view of the ball must be unobstructed to give him an opportunity to stop a direct shot. The inside forwards should mark the halfbacks immediately after the kick is taken.

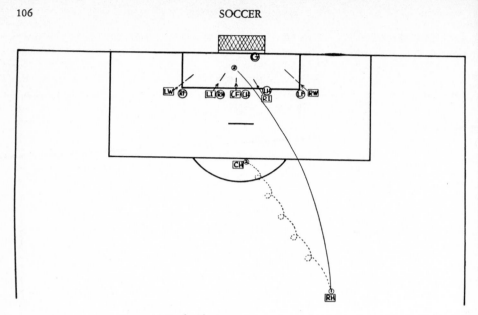

Backs playing too near the goal.

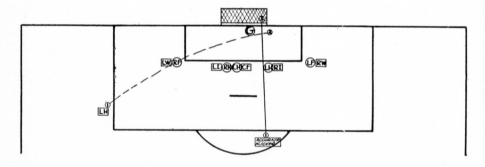

Backs playing correctly.

Penalty Kicks

When a major infracton of the rules is committed by a member of the defensive team in its own penalty area, the attacking team is awarded a penalty kick. This kick is taken from 12 yards directly in front of the goal. The only players allowed in the penalty area, or within 10 yards of the ball, when the kick is taken, are the kicker and the defending goalkeeper. The goalkeeper must stand (without moving his feet) on the goal line between the goal posts until the ball is kicked. The kick must be taken forward and may not be played again by the kicker until it has been touched by another player. In case the period ends after the penalty kick has been awarded but before it has been taken, extra time is allowed for the taking of the kick.

Penalty kicker.—He should be an accurate kicker and one with the ability to remain cool and relaxed under pressure. His duty is to score a goal, therefore he must keep the ball away from the goalkeeper and kick it hard enough to beat the goalkeeper's lunge. An instep kick moderately strong and aimed for the corner of the goal is probably the one most used.

If the kicker will stand to the left of and a few steps back of the ball so that a line drawn from him through the ball would enter the goal about one yard inside the goal post, he can use either the straight instep kick or the pivot kick with his right foot. This will disguise the direction of his kick until the last moment. He should have firmly fixed in his mind which kick he is going to use and not change his mind at the last moment, as this would probably lead to a kick straight at the goalkeeper.

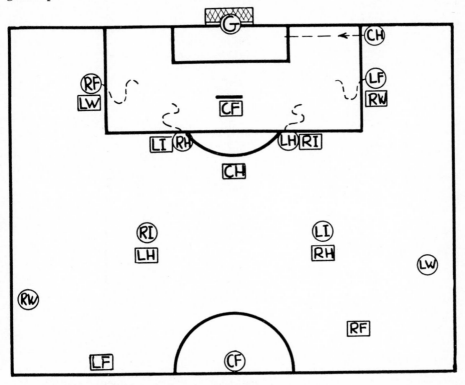

Good defensive but poor offensive positions.

Defensive duties.—The backs should play nearer the goal than the players they are marking. The inside forwards should mark the opponent's wing halfbacks. The defense should attempt to obstruct the run of the opponents to allow the goalkeeper more time to clear the ball in case of a partial stop or the ball hitting the cross-bar or goal posts.

The center half races in from the side to help clear any loose ball or to help defend the goal from a rebound shot. He then marks the center forward.

The wing forwards drop back to receive short clearing kicks or passes from the inside forwards.

Offensive duties.—The forwards attempt to play nearer the goal than the opponents marking them. The inside forwards take a stand where the arc meets the penalty area line, as from here they are one step ahead of their markers. The wing forwards are off-side unless the ball is played by the goalkeeper, and must cut

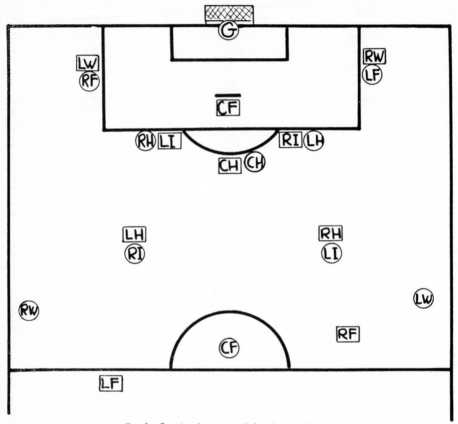

Good offensive but poor defensive positions.

back if the ball hits the cross-bar or goal posts, or is cleared by the goalkeeper in order to avoid a penalty. The inside forwards and center halfback play the ball provided it rebounds from the goal posts, as the kicker is not eligible for a second kick at the ball until it has been played by another player. The wing halfbacks play nearer the goal than their markers and together with the fullback nearest the goal cover any short clearances. The other fullback marks the opponent's center forward. When a player, other than the center forward, takes the kick, the center forward changes positions with him.

SUGGESTIONS FOR THE REFEREE

Before the Game

Arrive on the field well before game time.

See that: the field is properly marked, the corner flags are proper height or not dangerous.

Check the nets for holes and to be sure it is sufficiently pegged down.

Find out from the managers or coaches the agreed-upon length of periods or other changes in the rules, such as: charging of the goal-keeper and substitutions.

If you have reason to doubt the legality of the players' shoes or are requested to do so, examine them.

See that the linesmen are ready with flags and understand their duties.

Call the team captains to the center for the toss before game time.

Furnish a coin for the toss. Make note of the team kicking off.

Instruct captains of any agreed upon changes of the rules.

Note which players are acting as goal-keepers. They must wear different colors from the other players.

Write down the time the game started and when the first period will end.

During the Game

Anticipate the course of the ball. It helps you to keep up with the play.

Watch the players rather than the ball, since the players do the infringing.

Be keen to detect and call the first infringements of the rules. This gets you off to a good start and makes control of the rest of the game easier.

When you blow your whistle, blow hard and short.

Be absolutely fair and impartial in every decision.

Once given, do not change the decision.

Remember that you should not call infringements where by so doing you would be penalizing the wrong team. Call "PLAY ON."

Know the nine offences for which a penalty kick may be awarded. Note that all nine require that the offence be INTENTIONAL.

When you call an infringement and award a kick, hurry to place the ball where the infringement was made, indicate the direction of the kick, and run to get into position. As you arrive near this position blow the whistle for the taking of the kick.

See that free kicks are taken promptly after the whistle has blown.

When cautioning a player, call him by or require his name and tell him that if he again infringes he will be ordered off the field. Make note of his name.

Indicate clearly the side from which the goal kick is to be taken.

If CERTAIN that the whole of the ball has passed over the goal line between the posts give a goal.

Make notes of the goals as they are scored.

When you see the ball and a player's hand meet, and in your opinion it was not intentional use of hands, call "PLAY ON." This notifies both sides that you have seen the play and have judged it unintentional.

QUESTIONS AND ANSWERS ON THE LAWS OF SOCCER

Questions (Answers on Page 114)

1. If an opponent is charged when not in possession of the ball, what is the punishment?
2. What should a referee do if a penalty kick has to be retaken and time expires before this can be done?
3. What should a referee do if the ball, which would have otherwise have gone out of play, strikes him and remains in play?
4. What is the penalty when a goalkeeper carries a ball for more than four paces in the penalty area?
5. How much of the ball should be over the goal line for the ball to be out of play?
6. A defending player is sent off the field for an offence committed after a corner kick has been given. How should the game be restarted?
7. If the referee discovered at the end of a period that he had not allowed minutes enough for that period, should he add minutes enough to the next period to make this time up?
8. A back, with his goalkeeper out of position heads the ball out, but in doing so falls into the net. A forward gets the ball and passes it to a comrade who has only the goalkeeper to beat. Is this player offside?
9. An inside forward standing shoulder to shoulder with the center-forward kicks off in a forward direction to his outside-left after the signal is given. Is this allowed?
10. May an attacker stand ten yards from the ball when a goalkick is taken?
11. A back in order to save a certain goal attempts to punch the ball out, but only succeeds in deflecting it, and it rolls slowly into the net. What is the decision?
12. A player standing outside the penalty area reaches out and handles the ball inside the penalty area. Would you give a penalty?
13. When kicking off, a player stabs the turf and the ball moves only a few inches and the same player kicks the ball again. What should the referee do?
14. A goal kick is taken and is sent direct to an opposing player standing in an offside position outside the penalty area, who nets the ball. Is it a goal?
15. A forward kicks the ball out of play at one end of the field. On turning around you see a defending player at the other end of the field in his own penalty area strike an opponent. What action would you take?
16. How would you penalize a goalkeeper for handling outside his own penalty area?
17. A player is just taking a penalty kick when you see one of his own side step into the penalty area. Would you stop the kick from being taken immediately?
18. If a player is in an offside position, does not interfere with play or seek to gain an advantage, would you give him offside?
19. What is the penalty for throwing an opponent by falling down in front of him?
20. Would a player be allowed to stand in an offside position at the taking of a penalty kick?
21. Can a player be offside from a drop ball by the referee?
22. A winger centers, but runs over the touch-line where he is fouled by an opponent. What should the referee do?

23. A winger, under the impression he has been fouled, retaliates with blows and the opposing back in his own penalty area catches the ball before play is stopped. What decision or decisions would you give?

24. Extra time is allowed for a penalty to be taken. The goalkeeper saves but deflects the ball on to the post, off which it rolls into the net. Would you allow a goal?

25. An indirect free kick is given and 13 players line up on the goal line between the posts. The ball glances off an attacker on the line on to a defender into the net. What is the decision?

26. A back and forward collide and the ball goes out of play. The back in getting up deliberately kicks the prostrate forward. What should the referee do?

27. The defending side is awarded a direct free kick outside the penalty area; the back takes the kick by passing back to his goalkeeper, who misses it and it goes into the net. Is it a goal? Give reasons for your answers.

28. What would be your decision given the same conditions as in question 47, except that the free kick is taken inside the penalty area?

29. A player is in an offside position standing in his opponents' penalty area and is fouled by a defender while the ball is in play. What is your decision?

30. The center-forward passes out to his right winger; at the moment the ball was last played the winger was standing level with an opposing back and had only one other defending player between him and his opponents' goal line, viz., the goalkeeper. Would you give the winger offside?

31. If your answer is "Yes" to the previous question, state reasons for your decision.

32. What is the award against a player who at a kick-off plays the ball backward?

33. Can a player be offside if he is in line with the ball when it is passed to him?

34. As the referee is about to blow for half-time a player crashes the ball into the net, but is given offside. A linesman convinces the referee at half-time that he has made a mistake with the offside decision. Can the referee award a goal?

35. An opposing forward and the goalkeeper collide, causing both to fall over the goal line. The ball remains in play, but the forward cannot get the ball because the goalkeeper has crossed his legs around the forward's ankle. What would you give?

36. The ball has crossed over the goal line outside the post when a defending back fouls an oncoming forward. What is the correct decision?

37. Should a goalkeeper wear a distinctive jersey?

38. The goalkeeper taking a goal kick in a high wind only succeeds in kicking it seven yards forward and it is blown back towards his own goal. A back, scenting danger, rushes across the goal and pushes the ball round the post. What decision should the referee give?

39. How far does the ball have to roll from a place kick before it is in play?

40. A defender in the penalty area, seeing a pass going to the opposing center-forward in an offside position, tries to stop the ball with his hand but only deflects it more favourably to the offside forward. What should the decision be?

41. With the knowledge of the referee, an injured forward goes into goal. A penalty is awarded later in the game. Can the original goalkeeper go back into goal for the penalty?

42. What is the penalty against a player who throws-in or kicks-in the ball and plays it before anybody else?

43. Can a player who takes a corner kick, which hits the goalpost and rebounds, play it again before it has been touched by another player?

44. What is the penalty for illegal obstruction?

45. When can a defending player stand within the ten yards limit while a free kick is to be taken?

46. What is the penalty against a player who takes a penalty kick and dribbles the ball before taking a shot?

47. What would you award if, at a throw-in, or kick-in, the ball went into the goal direct, i.e., without touching any other player?

48. Should a referee ever alter his award after he has restarted the game?

49. At a penalty kick the player kicks the ball back. What action, if any, would you take?

50. A team kicks off and by combined play manages to score without an opponent playing the ball. Would you award a goal?

51. Can a player carry the ball over the line and between the posts and below the crossbar and yet score a goal?

52. A goalkeeper saves but is pushed over by an oncoming forward. What is the penalty and where shall it be taken?

53. Can the goalkeeper standing outside the penalty area punch the ball and not be penalized?

54. Must all free kicks taken in the penalty area be kicked beyond the area before a second player can kick the ball?

55. Can a goal be scored direct by any player who gets the ball when dropped by the referee?

56. If the goalkeeper handled the ball outside the penalty area, what sort of kick would be awarded?

57. Can a player be off-side from a corner kick?

58. What action, if any, would you take if a team persistently kicked the ball out of play to deliberately waste time?

59. Can an attacking player stand inside his opponents' goal when a corner kick is being taken?

60. Is it a direct or indirect free kick if the goalkeeper carries the ball more than four paces in the penalty area?

61. When does the game actually commence?

62. The ball falls on the touch-line marking; is it out of play?

63. Would the following six questions count as goals? State "yes" or "no": Direct into the net from a corner kick?

64. Straight into opponents' goal from kick-off?

65. Direct into goal from a free kick for "off-side"?

66. A kick-in which the goalkeeper fields but allows to bounce out of his grasp?

67. A shot which hits the referee and is deflected past the goalkeeper into the net?

68. A shot taken by a player who puts the ball into the net when his own penalty kick shot has rebounded from the cross-bar No other player has touched the ball.

69. Can a corner flag-post be removed to allow a player to take a kick more easily?

70. Should a center-forward score a goal direct from a kick-off, what would the award be?
71. Can a player be off-side from a goal kick?
72. What action would be taken against a player who removes the flag at the taking of a corner kick?
73. An indirect free kick from an attacker goes straight into the goal. What is the award?
74. What would you do if a player at a drop-down played the ball before it touched the ground?
75. Would you take any action if a player took a direct free kick for "hands" backward?
76. A player remains in an off-side position all through the game. What is the penalty?
77. A goalkeeper runs out to the penalty spot to field a ball, but is promptly bowled over in a fair charge by an oncoming forward. What would you give?
78. A player in an off-side position on the penalty line stops a goal kick. Would you blow off-side?
79. When an indirect free kick given against a goalkeeper for carrying in his goal area is about to be taken, two of the defending side stand on their goal-line. Is this in order and, if not, what should be done?
80. An indirect free kick is given to the defence in their penalty area, and the back, in an attempt to kick the ball to his goalkeeper, sends it into the net. What decision would you give?
81. A player taking a penalty kick mis-kicks and the ball rolls only a few inches, but one of his own players rushes up and crashes it into the net. Is it a goal?
82. If a player went to the edge of the field of play for a drink, would you take any action?
83. What is the award if a defending goalkeeper rushes out as an opponent is about to take a penalty kick?
84. If a player accidentally touches the ball with his hand or arm, or trips an opponent, what is the award?
85. What would be the award if the ball strikes the referee and goes over the goal line?
86. What does the law say regarding a player who raises himself on to his toes while taking a throw-in?
87. After a stoppage through accident, how and where would the game be restarted?
88. A player complains five minutes before half-time that an opponent has metal toe-plates. Should the latter be ordered off to change his boots or could he be allowed to wait until the interval?
89. If a player retaliated with two blows after being hit and you saw both offences, what action should you take?
90. What award would you make for a technical offence?
91. The defending players cluster around you and protest after you have awarded a goal. What action would you take?
92. A player is hit by the ball in the stomach and falls to the ground rolling in apparent pain. What course will you adopt?

93. What action would you take if a player shouts "Right, it's mine" as he and opponent go for the ball?

94. What action would you take if an attacker encroached when a penalty kick is being taken and the ball does not go into the net?

95. Should every case of "hands" be penalized?

96. Just before a penalty kick is about to be taken, the goalkeeper moves from the right to left to put the kicker off. What action would you take if the ball went between the posts?

97. What is the penalty if a player leaves the field without permission?

98. A defender within the penalty area stumbles in his efforts to clear the ball, but he pushes out his hand deliberately and stops the ball on the penalty line. What should the decision of the referee be?

99. Two players kick the ball at the same time, and the ball goes out of play. Whose throw-in or kick-in is it?

100. What award would you give if a goalkeeper in trying to catch a high ball raises his knee into the abdomen of an opponent?

101. Can a goal be scored direct from a free kick awarded for off-side?

102. Can a free kick, other than a penalty for an infringement, be awarded against the defending side in their penalty area?

103. Taking a penalty spot kick, the kicker passes the ball backwards to one of his own side, who immediately puts the ball into the net. Give your decision and the reason for it.

104. The goalkeeper is beaten by a shot, but before the ball can cross the goal-line, a spectator leaps on the playing-field and saves a certain goal. What is your decision?

105. State nine technical infringements which are punishable by free kicks from which goals may not be scored direct.

106. A player taking a throw-in takes a preliminary run, drags his back foot on the throw but keeps both feet behind the side-line and a part of each in contact with the ground until after the ball leaves his hands. Do you take action?

107. Name 7 times that a player can not be off-side.

108. A player kicks at a ball held in the goal-keeper's hands, what is the award?

109. Must a charge to be fair always be shoulder to shoulder?

110. The goal-keeper while bringing his arm back to throw the ball, holds it momentarily over the goal-line and between the posts. Do you award a goal?

111. A player kicks the ball in the air over the side-line. The wind blows it back so that it lands in the playing field. Do you take action?

Answers (Questions on Page 110)

1. An indirect free kick.
2. Time is allowed for kick to be retaken.
3. Drop ball.
4. An indirect free kick.
5. The whole of the ball must be over the line.
6. Take the corner kick.
7. No.
8. No. The back is still in the net.

9. Yes.
10. Law 16 has been changed to read that all opponents must stand outside the penalty area.
11. A goal.
12. Yes, unless it was the goal-keeper who has handled or one of the opponents.
13. Kick-off again.
14. Yes. No player can be off-side on a goal kick.
15. Take the defender's name, order him off and restart the game with a goal kick, throw-in, or kick-in.
16. A direct free kick.
17. No Retake if goal is scored, otherwise allow play to go on.
18. No.
19. A direct free kick.
20. Yes. But would be given off-side if the kick failed to score and the player moved to interfere with the game.
21. No.
22. Allow play to go on if a goal is likely to be scored. If not, stop play, caution infringing player and drop the ball where it was when play stopped.
23. Send off the striker and give a penalty for handling.
24. A goal.
25. Off-side.
26. Send the offender off; resume the game with a throw-in, kick-in, goal kick, or corner kick.
27. A corner kick. Direct free kicks can only be scored against the offending team.
28. Retake the free kick. Ball must go beyond penalty area.
29. A penalty.
30. Yes.
31. Because at the time the ball was last played he had only one man between himself and the goal line, being level with a man does not count.
32. Retake the kick.
33. No.
34. No. Lineman should speak to referee immediately.
35. A penalty kick.
36. Caution or order the player off. Restart the game with a goal or corner kick.
37. Yes.
38. Kick to be retaken.
39. Its full circumference.
40. Off-side, if the center-forward attempted to receive the ball at the moment it was passed.
41. Yes.
42. Indirect free kick.
43. No.
44. An indirect free kick.
45. When standing on his own goal-line between the goal-posts.
46. Indirect free kick for playing the ball twice.
47. Either a corner or goal kick.

48. No.
49. Indirect free kick to the defending team.
50. Yes. It has been played by a second player.
51. Yes. If it was the goal-keeper or a defender.
52. A direct free kick from where the ball was when the game was suspended.
53. Yes. If the ball is within the area.
54. No. Kicks taken by the attacking team are not included.
55. Yes. Provided it has touched the ground first.
56. Direct free kick.
57. No.
58. Caution the player concerned and allow for the time wasted.
59. No.
60. Indirect free kick.
61. When the ball has rolled its complete circumference.
62. No. It must be completely outside the line.
63. Yes.
64. No.
65. Yes.
66. Yes.
67. No.
68. No.
69. No.
70. A goal kick.
71. No.
72. Caution him and have flag replaced before kick is taken.
73. Goal kick.
74. Redrop.
75. No; unless it was a penalty kick which must be taken forward.
76. None, unless he interferes.
77. Nothing (international). Forward out of game (NCAA).
78. No. Retake the goal kick.
79. Is in order, if defenders are on goal-line and between goal-posts.
80. Kick to be retaken.
81. No. Retake.
82. No.
83. Retake penalty kick if goal is not scored.
84. None. Play on.
85. Drop ball.
86. Part of each foot shall be on the ground on or behind the side-line.
87. Drop the ball from the spot where the game was stopped.
88. Send him off to change his shoes.
89. Send both players off.
90. An indirect free kick.
91. Issue a caution and send off players on repetition.
92. Stop the game if a player is seriously injured.
93. Indirect free kick for ungentlemanly conduct.
94. Allow play to proceed.

95. No. Only if intentional.
96. Award a goal.
97. Indirect free kick.
98. A penalty kick.
99. Neither. The referee should drop the ball.
100. An indirect free kick for dangerous play.
101. No.
102. Yes.
103. Indirect free kick for not kicking the ball forward.
104. You cannot award a goal as the ball had not crossed the goal-line. Drop the ball at the spot it was played by the spectator (international).
105. (a) Goal-keeper carrying more than 4 steps.
    (b) Charging goal-keeper at wrong-time; the charge being otherwise fair.
    (c) Ungentlemanly conduct.
    (d) Persistently infringes any laws.
    (e) Dangerous play or dangerous conduct.
    (f) By word or action dissent from any decision.
    (g) Offside.
    (h) Penalty kick not kicked forward.
    (i) Playing the ball twice from throw-in or kick.
106. No. Meets all rules for throw-in.
107. When ball was last played:
    (a) In own half of field.
    (b) Two defenders between himself and goal-line.
    (c) Behind or level with the ball.
    (d) Goal kick.
    (e) Corner kick.
    (f) Throw-in (international).
    (g) By an opponent.
    (h) Drop ball.
108. An indirect free kick—dangerous play.
109. Yes.
110. Yes, if you are in position to see ball completely over line.
111. Yes, ball if completely over the line whether in air or on ground is out of play.

CHAPTER VIII

Team Offense and Defense

Systems of attack are based on the ability to retain possession or control of the ball, for, when a team has control of the ball, the opponents cannot score. The short passing attack is based upon the premise that the shorter the pass the less chance for inaccuracy or interception, while the long passing game is based upon the expectation of gaining great amounts of ground and many scoring opportunities through suddenness and speed of attack. The system of attack will depend primarily on the skill of the players and the number of better than average players on the team. The style of attack should be chosen to fit the players rather than trying to make the players themselves fit into a particular system.

Any system of attack should be in depth or waves of attackers and should attempt to cover as much of the offensive territory with players as is possible.

Defensive formations are so planned that there will be one extra defensive player to meet the point of attack or to back-up the other defensive players. The simpler the defense the easier it is to coach and the easier it is for the players to visualize and master. For this reason many coaches prefer the man-for-man defensive formation where each player's assignment is specific.

It is necessary for players to direct the play of each other. To avoid confusion the coach should set up some system whereby the players will know who is to call the play or the pass. In most cases this should be the key man or the man in the best position to see the field of play. An example of this would be:

The goalkeeper directs the backs when the play is near the goal.

The center halfback directs the halfbacks around the center of the field.

The wing halfbacks direct the inside and wing forwards on the attack. Provided the halfback is not up with the play, the wing directs the inside forward when the inside has the ball, and vice versa.

The center forward directs the play when the ball is near the opponent's goal.

When the directions are in words such as "center," "wing," or "cross," the opponents will know where the ball is going and can move to intercept it. To avoid this, some system of signals must be worked out whereby key words or numbers are called.

The Long Passing Attack

The attack attempts by long sweeping passes to use the speed of the wing forwards to unbalance the defense, and calls for players who can kick hard and with some degree of accuracy. It will work well against a team that plays its fullbacks in a straight line with each other or against a defense that leaves the opposite wing unmarked. The attack calls for the center forward to play as near the opponent's goal as possible and still remain on-side. It is varied by attempts to make long

118

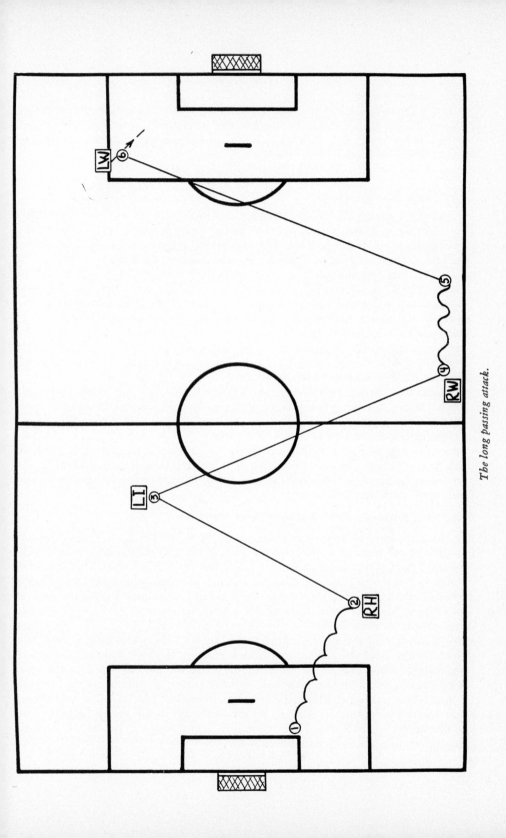

The long passing attack.

kicks up the center to the center forward who may attempt to beat his marker or may pass to the wing.

When the forwards are near the opponent's goal and the ball is cleared by the defense, they remain and wait for the backs to set the ball up in front of the goal.

This attack works well with the wind or on wet ground where any mistakes or mis-kicks by the opponents can be taken advantage of at once. It does not require as much ball control as the short passing system of attack.

The Short Passing Attack

The attack attempts by means of short passes to advance the ball surely and safely down the field. Passes are seldom over fifteen yards in length and are alternated by dribbles when that is possible. The preference, however, is for the pass, as it is the best means of beating an opponent and the surest way to keep possession of the ball. The short passing game demands accurate handling of the ball over short distances, good surface conditions of the field, and cool, heady play. A team trained in the short pass attack will often play better against the wind than with it.

Beginners have a tendency to close in on each other and bunch when learning and must be cautioned about it, as one defender can take the ball away from two or three attackers that are bunched.

As the ball is hard to control on a muddy or uneven field, this type of attack calls for more skill under these conditions.

Teams that depend on the long passing attack will find themselves in trouble when playing against a strong wind and therefore should receive some training in the short passing game.

Regardless of the type of attack, the players must be drilled in some kind of offensive formation so that they will know where their teammates will be at all times. The choosing of this formation will depend to a large extent upon the number of good players available, as each formation has certain key positions, and some have more than others.

The "W" Formation with Roving Center Halfback

The forwards and backs play in the shape of a "W." The two wing forwards and the center forward are the first wave of attack with the inside forwards backing them up, and they in turn being backed-up by the three halfbacks. This formation works better if the center halfback is allowed to roam around the field on the attack. He might even at times be in the forward line or shooting for the goal on back passes from the center forward. He acts as the intermediary between the two inside forwards when the ball is to be crossed from one side of the field to the other.

The strength of the attack is through the center of the field with the center forward, inside forwards, and center halfback carrying the ball. Provided the defensive players are drawn to the center of the field, the ball is passed to the open wing, who may dribble down the side line and center; or dribble toward the goal. When a long passing attack is used with this formation, the "W" is usually deeper with the inside forwards coming up as fast as possible as the goal is neared.

The center halfback marks the opponent's center forward, but as the halfback may be up field on the attack, the fullbacks must also keep an eye on this player.

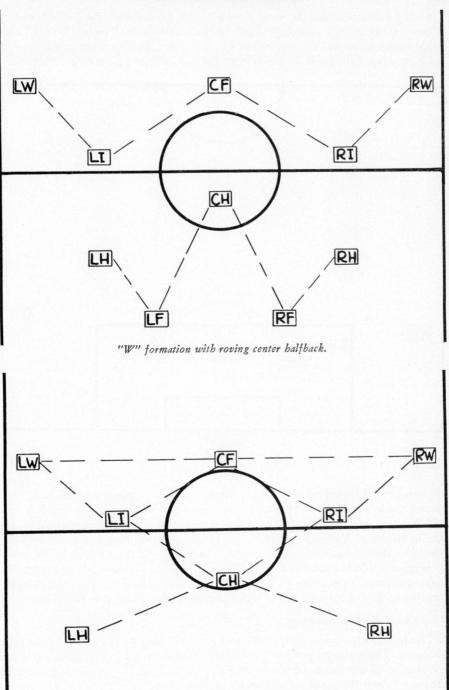

"W" formation with roving center halfback.

Possible passing combinations.

The wing halfbacks mark the wing forwards, and the fullbacks the inside forwards. When the center half cannot get back to mark the center forward, he marks the inside forward that has the ball and blocks that player from passing to the opposite inside or wing. This gives the inside with the ball only one place to pass it, namely,

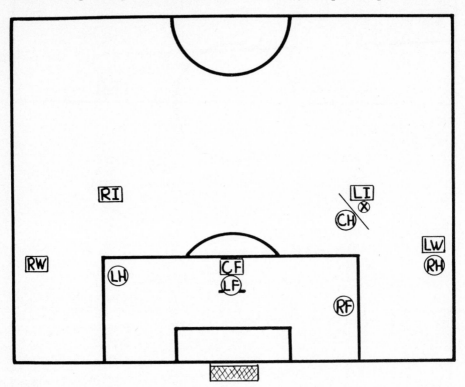

Center halfback forcing play to the strong side.

his own wing forward who is already marked. The example shows the center half forcing the left inside with the ball to the strong side of the defense. The left halfback has two men to mark, but as a pass to either of these players must be a long one, he should be able to intercept it. The inside forwards mark any of the opposing team's halfbacks that come up to support the attack. As the strength of the attack or defense depends upon the roving halfback, he must be an excellent player. The defense shifts to concentrate its power on the attacking side and therefore is a combination of a man-for-man and a zone defense, as the marking is not close.

The Third Back Formation

The forwards play in a deep "W" and are backed up on the attack by the wing halfbacks. These players position themselves near the center of the field, slightly to the outside of the inside forwards, and may move either in or out in backing up the line. When the short passing attack is used, they form triangles for combination play with the wing and inside forward or with the inside and center forward.

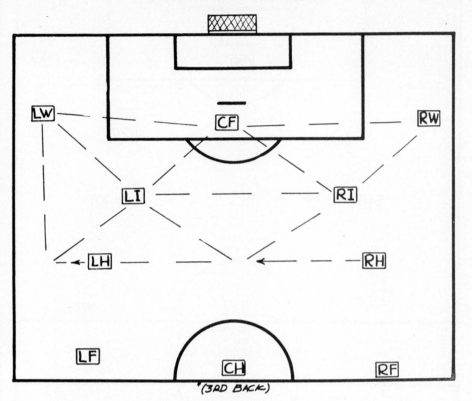

Passing combinations and wing half-back shift.

When one wing half moves out toward the side line, the other one moves toward the center of the field. If one moves over behind the center forward, the other drops back, and the fullback on the side of the field left open moves up to cover this space.

The wing halfbacks are used to receive passes when the forwards meet strong resistance, and then may dribble until one of the forwards is left open for a pass.

A pass from one wing halfback to the other is often used to switch the ball from one side of the field to the other and open up the play. The key men in the formation are the inside forwards and the wing halfbacks, who must be exceptionally good. The attack has two strong points, one on either side of the field, but is weak in the center.

The center halfback, playing as the third fullback, has only one duty and that is to nullify the play of the opponent's center forward. It calls for very close marking at all times and wherever the center forward plays. Either a man-for-man or a zone defense may be used with the third back formation. When a man-for-man defense is used the wing halfbacks mark the inside forwards, and the fullbacks the wings. When the defense is set, the fullback farthest from the play moves toward the center of the field to be ready to tackle any opponent breaking by a defender. The inside forwards mark the opponent's halfbacks.

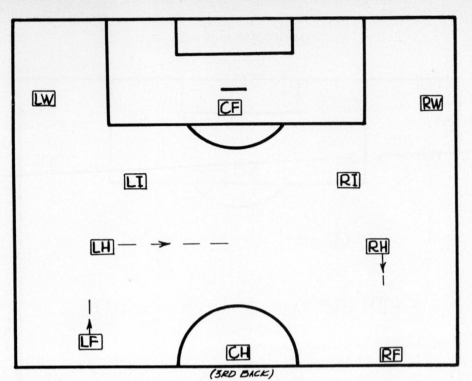

Halfback and fullback switch.

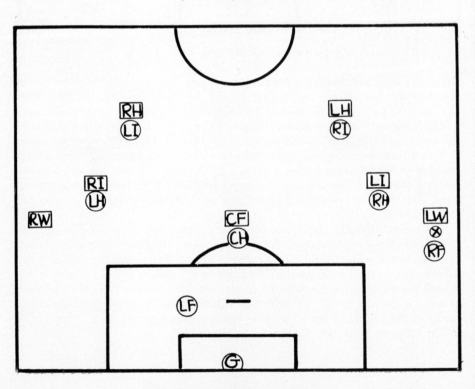

Third-back and man-for-man defense.

When a zone defense is used the backs on the side on which the attack is developing move up to meet it, while the backs on the far side move back. The center halfback still plays the center forward.

If the ball is moved to the other side of the field, the wing halfbacks pivot on the center halfback to meet the new attack. The halfback on the far side has two men to watch, as the left fullback has moved over to make the extra defensive man.

When the play develops in the center, it is up to the center halfback to force it to one side or the other so that the other backs will know how to shift.

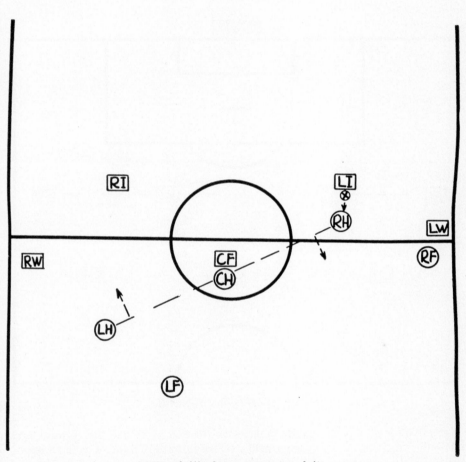

Wing halfbacks pivot on center half.

Defensive Center Forward Formation

The formation calls for the center forward and center half to drop back one position, so that the team has four forwards, three halfbacks and three fullbacks. It works well on a narrow field where often there is not sufficient room for five forwards to maneuver. All three of the halfbacks follow the forwards in on the attack, forming five triangles for a short passing game.

On the defense the center halfback marks the opponent's center forward, the fullbacks mark the wings, and the wing halfbacks mark the inside forwards. The defense can thus be played as shown for the third back formation.

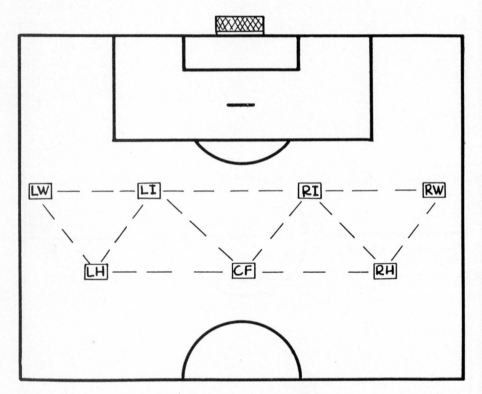

Defensive center forward formation.

A variation of this defense is to have two halfbacks follow the forward line while the third one covers the opponent's center forward. On the defense all opponents are closely marked with the wing fullbacks taking the wings, the halfbacks taking the center and inside forwards, while the center fullback acts as a roving safety man.

SANE SOCCER FOR ELEMENTARY SCHOOLS

Soccer is a grand game for all people at any age, but this does not mean that at all ages the international rules need be followed to the exclusion of common sense.

Simple reasoning should lead us to the conclusion that for elementary pupils a field of 120 yards by 75 yards is too large for the running ability of the participants; that a ball 28 inches in circumference weighing 15 ounces and inflated to a pressure of 13 pounds is too large and heavy; that goals eight feet in height and 24 feet in width are out of proportion to the size of the player; and that a game of four 22 minute periods is too long and a rest of 10 minutes between the halves too short.

Many teachers and coaches realize the importance of some of these factors but not all of them. Most have shortened the length of the game and the size of the field, but have overlooked two other important factors: size of ball and size of goal.

As there is no official soccer ball for midget and junior players individual judgement must be used in selecting the ball to be used. There are various sized playground balls of rubber, some having leather covers, which have sufficient weight to enable them to be controlled on a windy day, and yet light enough to suit the size of the players.

A goal 6 feet high and 18 feet wide would seem to be about the maximum size for midget and junior players. Reduction of the size of goal and field should be followed by reduction of the goal and penalty areas, and reduction of the distance between the goal line and the penalty kick mark.

The following deviations from international rules is recommended for elementary grade soccer games:

Size of field: 50 yards in width, 75 yards in length (see diagram 1 page 10) or adapted to the school playground as long as the length is greater than the width.

Size of goals: 6 feet in height, 18 feet in width (maximum).

Ball: One-half to two-thirds of official size and weight, 8 to 10 pounds pressure.

Time of game: 4 periods of 10 minutes each (maximum) with 15 minutes between halves and 5 minutes between periods 1 and 2, and 3 and 4.

Penalty kick mark: 10 yards from goal line.

Penalty area: 15 yards from each goal post and 15 yards into field of play.

Goal area: 5 yards from each goal post and 5 yards into field of play.

SWITCH PLAYS

A switch play is one in which the players deliberately go out of position or exchange places. It is used to confuse or upset the opponent's defense or to gain a fast break. It is more effective against a team playing a two-back game than against a three-back defense.

The following are examples of some of the common and simple switch plays.

Against a man-for-man defense, have the inside and outside forwards line up in each other's position at the opening kick-off. This may cause temporary confusion in the defense, for they will be marking the wrong man.

Against a man-for-man defense, when the ball is near the opponent's goal, the outside passes to his inside and cuts closely behind him for a return pass and shot. The outside should gain a stride on his guard because the inside and his guard form a screen to obstruct the outside's guard.

Against a zone defence, switch plays are used to overload a zone. This is best done by moving the center forward into the inside forward's zone. If the defender of the center zone moves to the new zone, he leaves the front of the goal wide open. If he does not move then the offense has two forwards against only one defender.

A fast break from the center of the field can be gained by the center forward passing to the outside forward who is cutting diagonally toward the center of the field. After the pass the center forward cuts diagonally toward the outside of the field.

A fast break can also be secured when the wing has the ball near mid-field. The center forward cuts diagonally forward to that side of the field for a through pass down the sideline. When the pass has been made, the wing cuts diagonally forward into the center forward position.

When either a halfback or fullback has possession of the ball he should move it forward. If no opposition develops, he should keep on dribbling the ball until he draws an opponent to him. This will cause a switch, for someone in the forward line must drop back to cover his position.

The players on teams using switch plays must be experienced enough to realize that the switch is only temporary and that all positions must be covered as soon as possible. They must also show good sense in picking the time to switch back to their own position. Switch plays used by inexperienced players can do more harm than good.

The defense against switch plays is for the backs to switch defensive assignments as they see the play develop. This is best done by having them call to each other to switch.

CHAPTER IX

Principles of Coaching

This chapter is aimed at the young coach or the coach who is meeting with little success. Admittedly it is difficult to adopt all the principles set forth. However, if one studies the methods of great coaches in any sport he will find that they use many or all of these principles.

Establish A Program That Will Develop Varsity Players

Any coach can have a good team once in awhile, but the coach who wants a good team every year, must establish a farm system.

The high school coach should attempt to get the fundamentals taught in the elementary grades gym periods. This could be formal instruction and/or the playing of games containing the fundamentals of soccer. He should attempt to get competition between grades and should start an elementary school league. This can be a modified game using a lighter ball, a smaller field, and shorter periods of time. See page 126. This plan of teaching and playing should carry over into the junior high school physical education program. He should also run a schedule of games between the playgrounds during the summer.

The college coach should try to get soccer into the intramural program. He should get at least a few games for his junior varsity, and freshman teams, and he ought to develop indoor soccer on a league basis to play during the winter months.

Keep As Many As Possible Out For The Team

Many coaches agree that what is taught one year does not really appear as a playing habit until the following year. Since no one can predict the speed of learning or the desire to learn, no one can predict from one year to the next who will improve enough to be of value to the first team. There is a definite correlation between the size of the squad and the success of the team. This is mainly due to the fact that the team is only as strong as its substitutes. The good team can replace injured players with almost-as-good substitutes, and the best teams have a second team almost equal to the first in playing ability.

In order to keep all the players interested it is necessary to divide them into groups or teams according to ability early in the season. Give them all a chance to scrimmage when it is not necessary for the first team to use the varsity field. Use seniors who are fair players but not good enough to make the first squad as coaches of these teams. If possible provide them with managers so that they get the feeling of "belonging."

Teach One Thing At A Time

Good teaching consists of presenting one thing at a time on which the pupil is to focus his attention. Rapid mastery of small skills is satisfying, encouraging to the player, and creates in him the desire to learn more.

When too many points are presented at one time the player can concentrate on none, and becomes confused. The result is slow learning.

Correct One Thing At A Time

When more than two faults at a time are pointed out to a player, it is apt to arouse his resentment. This is especially likely to happen if he is criticized before the whole team. He may lose his respect for his coach, become discouraged or lose his desire to make the team.

Correcting one thing at a time has the opposite effect. Now the players feels that he is on the verge of success and works hard to correct that fault. Having conquered that one, he does not seem to mind when another flaw is pointed out to him.

Be positive when you make your corrections. It is negative coaching to tell the player what not to do. It is positive coaching to tell and show him what to do.

Coach One Thing at a Time

This principle refers more to game situations than to fundamentals. Too many coaches try to coach too many things at one time.

To concentrate on coaching the defense, use a weak forward line and stay with the coaching of the defense. When the players become skilled against the weak forward line, put in a stronger line. Continue to add stronger lines until the defense is good enough to stop the best line.

Work On Fundamentals Again and Again

Coaches often lose sight of the relationship between learning and forgetting. The curve of learning goes up to a peak but unless the learning is reviewed the curve starts to decline. When a man has not practiced a skill for a period of time, he tends to become rusty. It is the law of disuse taking effect. The remedy is relearning or practice. Each skill should be practiced in a variety of drills so the players do not become bored and apathetic.

Review Fundamentals Once A Week

This principle is a sequel to the preceding one. Put emphasis on the fundamentals where players have demonstrated weakness. Admittedly both players and coach get bored with constant practice of fundamentals. The coach must overcome his own apathy and devise some means to overcome that of the players. Suggested methods are:

(1) Practice the fundamentals under game conditions. This creates a contest between players which disguises the objective.

(2) Use games and drills. See Appendixes 1 and 2.

(3) Have the better players coach the others. Assign one man from each of your other teams to each first string player. As the coach calls out the fundamental to practice, the varsity man reviews that point with his students. In doing so he will demonstrate and concentrate on perfect performance. And that is the coach's objective.

Evaluate The Fundamentals And Game Situations

Unless the coach has clearly in mind the value of each skill and team situation, he is quite apt to spend too much practice time on not-so-important items.

In general, the value of an item can be judged upon how often it occurs in a game. This is modified by its value in scoring or preventing a score. For example, kick-off plays occur only a few times in a game and rarely lead to a score, but throw-in or kick-in plays occur often in a game and therefore have more value in practice.

The steps in evaluation are two. First, make a list of all fundamentals and game situations. Second, assign percent value to each of these so that the total percentage equals one hundred. This will tell how much of the practice period to spend on each element of the game during the week.

If a given fundamental is valued at ten percent, then ten percent of the minutes in the practice period should be spent on this element.

Plan The Practice Periods

In planning the practice period the coach should keep in mind his three major goals. These are the development of skill, of good physical condition, and of speed.

The coach who does not plan his practice period is quite apt to use one drill so long that the players lose interest and, since he runs out of extemporaneous material, tends to scrimmage every night.

Using his percentage evaluation list he is ready to plan both pre-season and in-season practice periods. He should plan to keep all players busy all of the time.

The presentation of new material should come early in the practice period while the players are still strong. If a drill using a large amount of energy is followed by one using a small output of energy, players will stay strong for a longer period of time. This chance to recuperate should alternate with strenuous drills. Used together they will build endurance.

The coach will find that his *practice* plans will vary from year to year and even during the same year, for his players' rapidity of learning will vary. However, if it is a good one, his *master* plan will remain unchanged.

The thesis generally is held that relatively short and well distributed practice periods produce superior results to longer, though less frequent practices. If things are going badly with practice of one skill, don't "stick with it until we get it," but go on to another and come back later to the skill causing difficulty.

Most improvement will result when each man has the maximum number of chances to work with the ball in a given period of time. This means well-organized drills with many balls in use, and small groups for practice with a ball. Boredom results from standing in line waiting for a turn rather than from repetition of a skill.

Plan something new and something in review for each session.

Drills which involve several sequential skills will be more useful and economical of time than single-skill drills.

Mental practice, that is, thinking through skills, has a definite positive effect upon motor learning.

Conduct Practice Under Game Conditions

A game condition is a condition that actually exists in a game, and has the same factors. The coach may have taught the art of evading an opponent in slow motion or against passive resistance, but this is not the game condition. In the game condition it must be done quickly and against a skilled opponent. Therefore, it is necessary to practice this skill against determined opposition, such as will be met in the game.

It is not always possible to practice a fundamental under game conditions. When this occurs, the time element may be substituted with good results. Here the opponent is time rather than a player.

The coach who fails to call the fouls made by his better players in scrimmage destroys the game condition and will develop poor habits in his players.

Drills, contests, and lead-up games can all be evaluated quickly by how well they meet this principle.

A drill requiring the forwards to spend a lot of time on heading the ball up into the air is not a game condition. Nine out of ten times in a game the coach wants the forward to head the ball down to someone's feet or down into the goal, so that is what should be practiced.

Exercises to correct isolated weaknesses in one or two players, such as skipping rope to overcome awkwardness, have no place in the practice period. These should be outside assignments.

Practice At Top Speed

Players tend to take it easy or to slow up during practice. Skills performed during a game are not in slow motion but at top speed. When the players, who perform skillfully but slowly during practice, try to speed this skill up during a game, they encounter difficulty. The reason is that they have practiced one thing and now they are trying to do another, and they are not the same.

Teach More Than One Type Of Attack And Defense

While it is true that the coach must adapt his team style of play to the abilities of his players, it is also true that for best results he must readjust his team's style to meet the opponent's weaknesses.

If the opponent is a clever, short-passing but slow team, then the best attack is the fast-breaking, long-passing game. The defense should check closely and be man-for-man.

If the opponent is a long-passing fast team, but lacks skill, then a short passing game is the best offense. Defense should be of the third-back type with the third back deep in his own half of the field. The other two fullbacks can play either in the zone defense system or in the two-back system of defense.

Unusual weather conditions often call for a change of type of play. When playing against a very strong wind, a short passing attack combined with the defensive center forward formation defense is indicated. This gives a team a very strong defense, although a weak attack. Playing with a strong wind alters the type of play. Other conditions affecting play are a strong cross-field wind, rain, muddy field, frozen ground or snow.

Allow No Horseplay During Practice

The danger of allowing horseplay is possible injury to players and to their attitudes toward each other. Further, the coach will lose the attention of the players. Without their attention, nothing can be accomplished.

If the coach keeps the players busy with the learning process, and if he has made the practice period interesting, the idle time which breeds horseplay will never arrive.

Do Your Conditioning At The End Of Practice

Players learn easiest before they become tired. It follows that the teaching or coaching should come in the early part of the practice period, before fatigue sets in. After they become tired it is difficult for them to concentrate and difficult to hold their attention.

Have Players Know The Rules And Their Interpretations

Many college coaches assume that their players know the rules because they played the game in high school. But even if they know the laws of the game, they still might not know the interpretations of the laws. This knowledge is sometimes a deciding factor in a game. The lack of knowledge often takes a player's mind off the game when he is called by the referee for an infraction of a law of which he was ignorant. It is most important that the players know the off-side law.

Many successful coaches have found that the best place to teach rules is during practice or scrimmage. They call all violations and ask the violator what rule he broke and what the penalty is for his violation.

Use All Possible Precautions To Avoid Injury

Each season many teams with winning records lose games to inferior teams because of injuries to their key players. Injuries sustained by players during a game or practice cannot all be prevented, but they can be held to a minimum. The precautions taken by good coaches are mentioned herein to act as a check list.

The best possible safety equipment should be worn in practice as well as in the game.

Training rules which are simple, sensible and few in number should be suggested. These should all point toward better physical condition. Players in good physical condition are less liable to be injured or become ill than others.

A trainer should be appointed. If he is not qualified to take care of injuries, then he can assist the coach in this duty. His main function should be to make sure that the coach knows of any player's lack of top physical condition.

The players' confidence in the fairness of their coach must be built up so that they will tell him when they have colds or injuries.

The coach should realize that he is taking a risk when he plays an injured man. He could lose the player for the remainder of the season should the injury recur. If a substitute is not normally as good as the injured man, he still might be better than a handicapped player.

To leave excessively tired players in a game is dangerous. Most injuries occur either very early in the game or when players of both teams become fatigued.

When the score is high enough so that victory is assured, it is wise to take out key players. There is nothing to gain by playing them and everything to lose should they become injured.

As most of the playing rules are made to prevent injury, they should be enforced to the limit, both in practice and in the game. Only the best officials should be hired. See that the rules are enforced even during drills.

Watch carefully for signs of staleness and take proper precautions. A stale player is apt to be reckless and heedless of danger.

Keep practice games and scrimmages to a minimum, for this is where most injuries occur. Pre-season games must be used to pick the better players and locate weaknesses in individual and team offense and defense. After the season has started, the scheduled games will do this for the coach. If there is only one scheduled game in a week, then one long or two short scrimmages are indicated in practice. The remainder of the time could best be spent perfecting game situations.

Undertrain Rather Than Overtrain

An undertrained team is one that is near peak condition and could reach its peak of playing ability in a week of hard work. An indication of this condition is when the players are constantly asking for scrimmage, work hard at practice without urging, and continue to practice after the squad has been dismissed. A team that can be held just undertrained will finish the schedule playing better than it did in its early games.

An overtrained team is often called a team that has gone stale. The one is the cause of the other. Staleness can happen either to an individual or to a team. It is more likely to occur when the combined training and playing season covers more than two months, and the scrimmages are long and often. It is a mental rather than a physical condition.

Team staleness symptoms are: players will not take practice seriously, their playing ability falls off, they lose to a weak opponent, they become "fed-up" with the sport, and the thrill of competition has worn out for them.

The remedy is a drastic change from the weekly routine, such as dismissing practice early, or giving the team a day or two holiday. In no case should a team that has gone stale be bawled out by the coach or be forced to take more of the same medicine. They have already had too much.

Individual staleness symptoms are often some of the following: the player loses weight, skill, or interest, plays carelessly, moves slowly in practice, shows irritability, indulges in dirty play, loses his temper easily, finds fault with team-mates, gets into fights, or becomes a sore-head. The treatment is rest or change, and should be explained to the player so that he does not feel that he is being punished. He might be given two or three days off from practice to catch up on his studies, or he might sit on the bench for a part or all of a game.

A coach should be alert for symptoms of staleness during the last half of the season. He should realize that he is the cause of the staleness and should not blame the team or player. The good coach recognizes the symptoms and applies the cure before damage is done.

Make Use Of Charts And Movies

Because it is possible for a player's personality to influence the judgment of a coach, it is best to devise some means of getting the cold facts. A film of each game will show a player's weaknesses and strong points but will not enumerate them.

Charts, on the other hand, enumerate cold facts. A partial chart might be:

Passes: completed
        intercepted
        not completed

Tackles: successful
         missed

Took ball: past an opponent
            failed to get past an opponent

Missed shots: over the crossbar
              outside near goalpost
              outside far goalpost

Charts can be scored during a game or scrimmage by second-string players, assistant managers, or injured players. The chart is apt to lose validity if one person is asked to score more than two players. Single charts are best but a fullback and a forward on the opposite side of the field can be combined satisfactorily.

Grow Professionally

Since competition gets better every year and the opposing teams' coaches get better, it is necessary for the man who wants successful teams to increase his knowledge of the game, and his ability to get the best performance out of his players.

He should read carefully all books on his sport; take summer courses in coaching; attend clinics and conventions; join the National Soccer Coaches Association; see professional teams play; play better teams; and seek the referees' opinions on players and team.

Complete knowledge of the sport comes from three sources: playing, coaching and refereeing. If a coach knows only the playing and coaching point of views, he should join a referees' group and do some officiating.

He should develop some showmanship on and off the field; a nickname helps, or an unusual hobby or method of acting. Whatever it is it should be dignified and printable in the newspapers.

It would be advantageous to him to take courses in psychology and apply them to his players and contemporaries. The coach who applies the correct psychology to his team is the one whose teams play an inspired game rather than a mechanical one.

He should write articles on his sport for magazines, for they are a sign of the coach's growth and actually will cause growth.

Finally, the time will come when the coach will be asked to speak at lunches, dinners, and banquets. He should prepare rough outlines of a few interesting topics; listen to good after-dinner speakers, and find out why they are considered good; write down humorous things that happen in practice and on trips; make note of funny stories; and then he will be prepared when the invitation to speak is extended.

Glossary

Active resistance—To forcefully oppose.

Angle of possibility (of possible shot)—That angle formed by imaginary lines drawn from each goal post to the ball and within which the ball must travel in order to enter the goal.

Backs—The half and fullbacks.

Back-up—To assume a position behind a teammate for the purpose of receiving a pass or of strengthening the defense.

Beat—To out-maneuver an opponent by either getting the ball behind him to a teammate or by getting behind him with the ball. Putting an opponent out of the play.

Center—To move the ball to the center of the field, usually in front of the goal.

Center circle—A ten yard radius circle drawn in the exact center of the field.

Center line—A straight line connecting the two side lines midway between the goal lines.

Charge—To use any part of the upper shoulder against an opponent to unbalance him.

Clear—To move the ball away from the scoring area near the goal.

Corner kick—A direct free kick given the offensive team, taken within one yard of the corner of the field.

Cover—To guard an opponent by remaining near him. The guarding is not as close as marking.

Cross—To move the ball from one side of the field to the other.

Direct free kick—A place kick which results in a score when kicked into the goal.

Draw a back (an opponent)—To induce an opponent to leave the player he is marking to mark the player with the ball.

End line—The boundary line marking the narrow end of the field.

Dribbling—To advance the ball by using the feet while keeping the ball within one stride.

Drop ball—A means of putting the ball in play after temporary suspension.

First-time kick—To kick a ball without first trapping it.

Goal area—That portion of the field enclosed by lines drawn six yards into the field from points six yards outside the goal posts.

Goal kick—An indirect free kick taken by the defensive team within that half of the goal area nearest to where the ball crossed the goal line.

Goal line—The line marking the narrow end of the field.

Half-volley kick—To kick a ball the instant after it touches the ground.

Head—To hit the ball with the head.

Hands—Intentionally touching the ball with any part of the arms or hands.

Holding—Obstructing a player's movement with hand or arm.

Indirect free kick—A place kick from which a score can not be made until the ball is touched by another player.

Kick-in—The method of putting the ball in play when it goes out of play over the side line.

Kick-off—An indirect free kick used as a means of starting each period of a game or restarting the game after a score.

Lead—To pass the ball ahead of the receiver.

Liquid catch—Catching the ball with hands and fingers relaxed while the arms are drawn toward the body.

Loft—To raise the ball into the air.

Lunge—To take a long stride placing the weight on the foot moved.

Mark—To remain so near an opponent that his efforts to play the ball would be hampered or nullified.

Obstruct—To hamper the movements of an opponent by remaining in the path he wishes to travel.

Pass—To kick or head the ball to a teammate.

Passive resistance—Using little effort to oppose.

Penalty area—That portion of the playing field bounded by lines drawn at right angles to the goal line eighteen yards out from each goal post and eighteen yards into the playing field. (International.)

Penalty kick—A direct free kick taken from the penalty mark.

Penalty mark—A point twelve yards directly in front of each goal usually indicated by a short line.

Place kick—A kick at a non-moving ball placed on the ground.

Punt—To kick a ball as it is dropped from the hands.

Play them off-side—A means of making the offensive players move away from the goal.

As the defensive players move away from the goal, the offensive players must do the same or they will be in an off-side position.

Save—To prevent a goal by intercepting the ball.

Scoring chance—An opportunity to take a shot at the goal.

Screen—To obstruct an opponent's view of the ball.

Set up (to set the ball up)—To kick the ball in the air so that it will land near the goal.

Side line—The boundary line marking the long side of the playing field.

Skied—A ball kicked unnecessarily high in the air.

Stalemate—Two players face each other and each waits for the other to make a move.

Stance—The position of a player's feet.

Stop—The catch or deflection of a shot by the goalkeeper. Usually used in referring to the number of times the goalkeeper prevented a score.

Strong foot—The foot with which the player is most proficient.

Trap—To stop the ball near the feet.

Tackle—To attempt to get the ball away from an opponent, to make him lose control of it, or to cause him to hurry his pass.

Volley—To kick a ball that is in the air at any time other than the instant after it touches the ground.

Weak foot—The foot with which the player has the least skill.

Wing forwards—The forwards nearest the side lines.

Wing halfbacks—The halfbacks on either side of the center halfback.

Drills on Fundamentals
Games to Make Practice Fun

Drills on Fundamentals

INSTEP KICKING DRILLS

1. Parallel Lines Drill

"LEG AND ANKLE RELAXED"

Divide the players into two parallel lines facing each other about fifteen yards apart with five yards between individuals in each line. Practice kicking at first for form and, as the lines move farther apart, secondly for distance. Repeat using the weak foot. Trap the ball before kicking.

2. Receive and Shoot Drill

"BODY OVER BALL"

FILE 1.   FILE 2

Divide players into two files and number the files 1 and 2. The first man in file number 1 passes ball to the first man in file number 2 who shoots for the corner of the goal. 2 retrieves ball and goes to the end of number 1 file. Number 1 goes to the end of number 2 file. The second pair of players should start when the ball has been played by the first number 2. Start the kick soon enough to meet the ball as it comes under the body.

3. First-Time Kick Drill

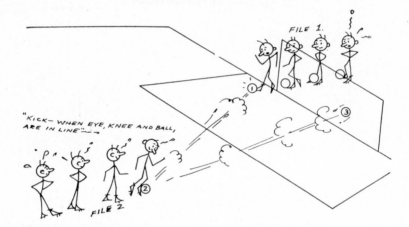

Use one ball to each pair of players. 1 passes to 2 who shoots at goal with instep kick. Repeat with 2 passing to 1. Keep the ball low by kicking it as it comes under the body. Relax the ankle.

4. Long Kick Drill

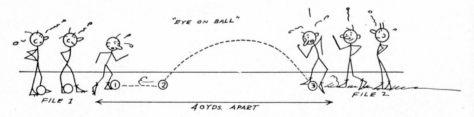

1 pushes ball in direction of 2 and then kicks it. 2 traps ball and repeats same. Place the non-kicking foot ahead of the ball and meet it as it comes alongside. Use parallel line formation.

5. Free Goal Shooting Drill

Players alternate with partner in shooting at goal. Use one ball to every pair of players. Emphasize shooting with accuracy from various distances and angles. Use the weak as well as the strong foot.

6. Center and Shoot Drill

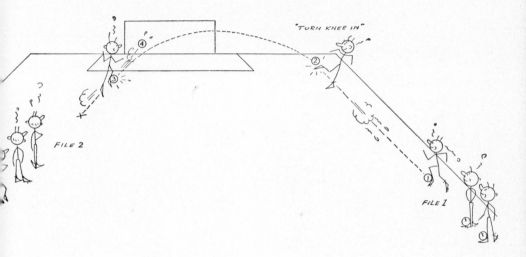

1 dribbles down side of field and centers to 2, who shoots for goal. 1 uses right-foot pivot kick. 2 has choice of using outside of right foot or left-foot pivot kick. 2 retrieves ball and goes to end of file 1. After centering 1 falls-in on end of file 2.

Note.—Pivot kicks are called right or left according to which foot kicks the ball, i.e., right-foot pivot kick, right foot meets the ball.

7. Corner Kick Drill

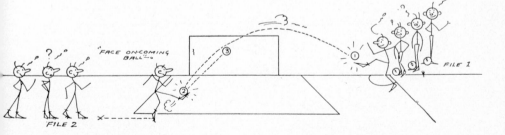

1 kicks from corner aiming at six yard line; 2 runs in and shoots for goal. 1 uses a left-foot pivot and 2 uses a right-foot pivot kick. Rotate players from one file to the other.

8. Cross, Center and Shoot Drill

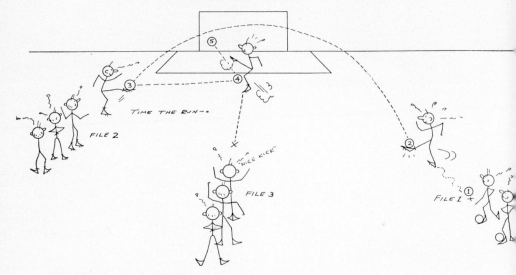

1 takes a short dribble and passes to far corner to 2, who centers ball for 3 to shoot. 1 uses right pivot, 2 uses left pivot, and 3 uses outside of left or right-pivot kick.

VOLLEY AND HALF-VOLLEY KICKING DRILLS

9. Volley Kick Drill

Practice in pairs. Have one player toss an easy ball to the kicker. Gradually increase the distance and height of the toss. Use the goal, a bank, or a bounding board to kick into or against.

10. Triangle Volley Drill

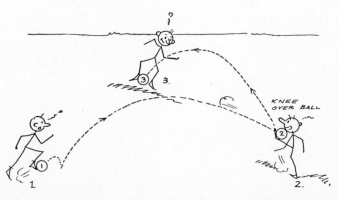

Practice in groups of three. 1 drop-kicks ball to 2, who volleys to 3. 3 drop-kicks ball to 1, who volleys to 2. Continue. Players start 15 yards apart and gradually increase distance.

11. First-Time Volley Drill

Parallel line formation. Drill 1.

Groups 1 and 2 volley back and forth across field. Use 2 men on each side of field per ball.

OVER-HEAD KICKING (LONG) DRILLS

12. Over-head Kick Drill

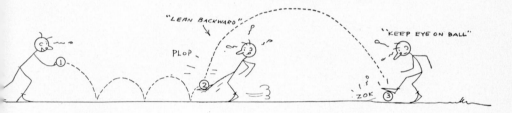

Work in groups of three. 1 bounces ball to 2, who over-head kicks to 3. 3 bounces ball to 2, who over-head kicks to 1. Change positions after every second kick.

13. Over-head Kick and Dodge Drill

1 throws ball over 2's head. 2 attempts to return the ball by an over-head kick on the first bounce. After ball leaves 1's hands. he rushes 2 and attempts to get the ball.

PASSING OR SHORT KICKING DRILLS

14. Two on One

1 passes to 2, who passes back to 1. 1 uses inside of left and 2 inside of right foot. 3 should stand still at first and then become more active in trying to stop the pass.

15. Pass Scoring Drill

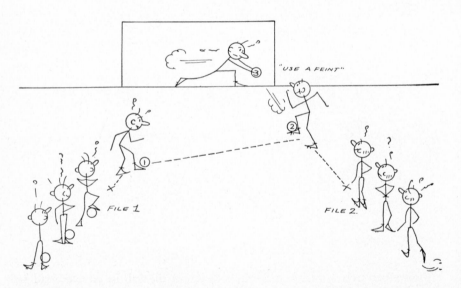

1 starts a dribble and with inside of left foot passes to 2, who tries to pass by the goalkeeper. Change drill by giving 1 the option of shooting or passing to 2.

16. Lob and Dodge Drill

Use Drill 13 formation. 1 bounces ball to 2 and follows up his throw in an effort to get the ball. 2 lob-passes over 1's head. More difficult: Use drop-kick in place of throw and lob before the ball bounces.

17. Throw-in and Lob Drill

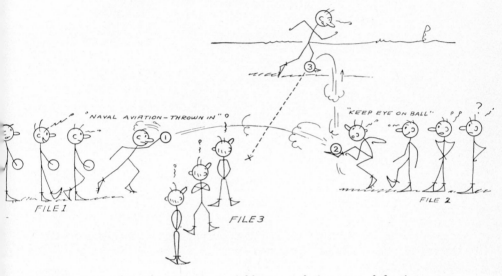

1 throws to 2 who lob-passes to 3. Add one and then two defensive men to give opposition.

18. Lob and Evade Drill

1 bounces to 2, who lob-passes over 3. 3 rushes 2 as soon as the throw is made, in an effort to get the ball. Start with passive and end with active resistance.

19. Three on Two Drill

"USE FIELD VISION"

1, 2, and 3 pass the ball back and forth as they run side-by-side down the field. Use inside and outside of foot passes with feints. Add defensive backs 4 and 5. Progress from passive to active resistance.

20. Blind Shooting Drill

FILE 3

FILE 2

"BE ANNOYING"

FILE 1.

3 passes ball across in front of goal. 2 runs along with 1 and attempts to obstruct 1's view of the ball by keeping in his line of vision and stepping over the ball at the last minute. 1 shoots for goal, retrieves the ball and goes to Line 3. 3 moves up to 2 and 2 goes to end of line 1.

21. Heel or Sole Pass Drill

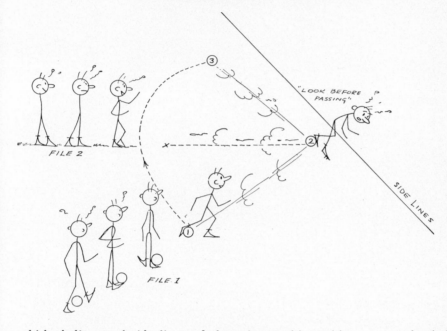

1 kicks ball toward side line and then changes his position. 2 runs for ball and passes it back to 1. 2 must look for 1 before he makes his pass. 1's kick should be fairly slow.

TRAPPING DRILLS

22. Deflection Trap Drill

Parallel line formation. 1 passes to 2 and runs forward to regain control of ball. 2 deflects ball to right or left in order to evade 1.

23. Trap Scoring Drill

2 throws to 1 near the goal post. 1 traps the ball into the net. Ball may be rolled, bounced or thrown in the air.

24. Deflection Trap and Dodge Drill

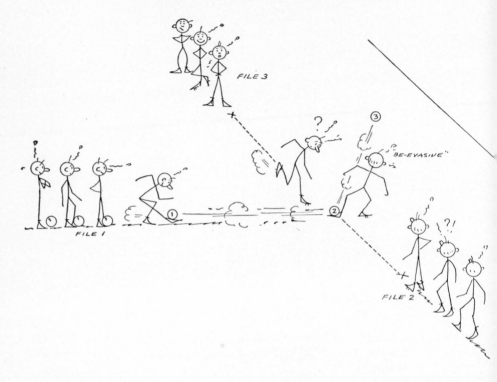

1 passes to 2, who is running. 2 must trap ball by 3, who is coming in to intercept. 3 at first must run in a straight line and slowly; later he may come in as he wishes, either cautiously or aggressively. Change angle of 1's pass to add variety.

HEADING DRILLS

25. Head and Dodge Drill

1 throws the ball to 2 and follows in to offer passive resistance. 2 heads the ball beyond 1 and attempts to recover it.

26. Head for Goal Drill

Drill 15 formation. 1 throws to 2 who heads the ball down for a shot at the goal. Vary the distance and the height of the throw to add judgment of speed and depth perception to the drill. May use goalkeeper.

27. Triangle Heading Drill

Drill 10 formation. 1 throws to 2, who heads to 3. 3 throws to 1, who heads to 2. Continue. Use with four men, to increase the heading angle.

BALL CONTROL DRILLS

28. Two Against Two Drill

One pair of players tries to keep the ball away from another pair. This is a very strenuous drill which will develop endurance as well as afford practice in passing, receiving, trapping, heading, marking, dribbling, tackling, charging, feinting, and use of pivots.

29. Playing the Ball Drill

The player attempts to keep the ball bouncing by playing it with his head, foot, or body between each bounce. He should vary the height of his kicks from low to fairly high ones, should vary the type of kicks to include inside of foot lob, instep kicks, and short over-head kicks, and should vary the direction of the headed balls.

TACKLING AND OBSTRUCTING DRILLS

30. Mass Tackling Drill

Parallel line formation. #1 players start dribbling from the side line on signal and are tackled by #2 players who are waiting at midfield. #2 players may continue attempts to obtain ball until 1's have reached the other side line. Continue with #2 players moving sideward one cadet so that they tackle a different #1 player each time.

31. Obstructing Drill

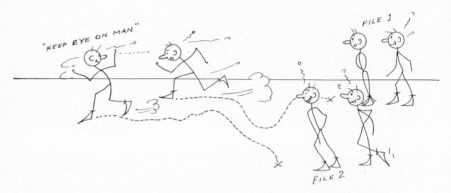

1 attempts to move along the side lines while 2 obstructs. (No ball.)

32. Backs Against Forwards Drill

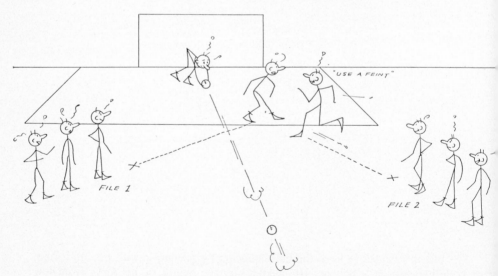

Place the backs in line 1 and the forwards in line 2. As the ball is rolled toward the goal, 1 and 2 start. 1 tries to cut in front of and obstruct 2 to enable G to get the ball.

GOALKEEPER DRILLS

33. CALLING FOR THE BALL DRILL

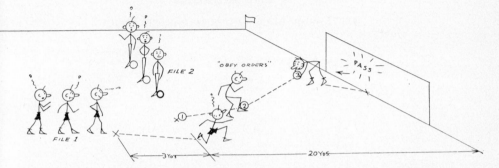

At the command "go" 1 and 2 start directly or diagonally toward the goal. 2 may try to trick 1 and turn the ball or on a call for the ball by the goalkeeper pass to him. 1 keeps after the ball. Passes to the goalkeeper should be made toward the outside of the nearest goal post.

34. STOPPING A DRIBBLER DRILL

Drill 35 formation. Player 1 dribbles toward the goal. The goalkeeper advances about six yards to narrow the angle of possible shot. 1 must be made to dribble at full speed as he would in this situation in a game.

35. STOPPING TWO MEN DRILL

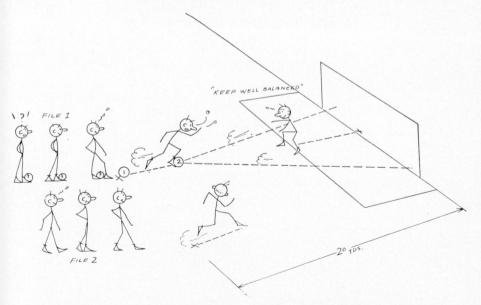

1 and 2 attack the goal at full speed. G should shorten the angle on 1 in case 1 tries to shoot. After shortening the angle he may try to feint 1 into passing. He

then has the choice of trying to intercept the pass, trying to reach 2 at the same time as the pass, shift to narrow the angle of 2's shot, or drop back to the goal line.

ATTACK DRILLS

36. THREE MAN QUICK-BREAKING DRILL

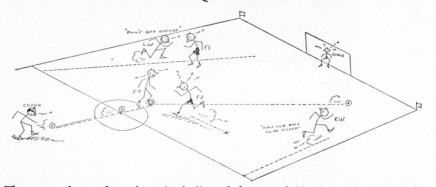

The center forward receives the ball, and draws a fullback to him by starting a dribble. If F-2 is drawn to him, he passes to R.W. toward the far corner, and sprints for the goal. L.W. cuts directly for the goal post on his side of the field. R.W. receives the ball and dribbles directly for the goal until he draws a back. He then passes to the unmarked forward. If he does not draw a back he should take a shot. Practice at top speed. Repeat drill against fullbacks playing in all possible defensive positions. Allow C.F. to attempt to beat his man and shoot when he has an opportunity.

37. FIVE MAN QUICK-BREAKING DRILL

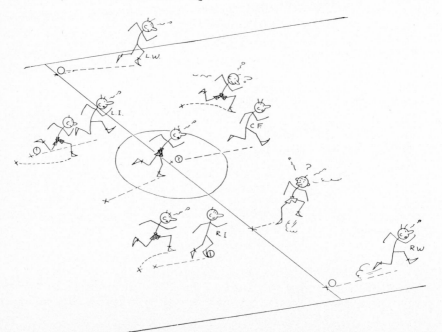

Each forward has a ball at his feet. The ball of the player named is in play. If the coach calls "right inside," the right inside's ball is in play and he immediately starts with a dribble or a pass. By giving the center and inside forwards a step or two advantage over the halfbacks all forwards are momentarily free to start an attack. Emphasize speed.

38. Two Men Combination Play Drill

Combination play *A* is a diagonal pass from one forward (1) to another (2). Combination *B* is a through pass by #1 and always made to the player calling it. Combination *C* is a backward pass by #1 to #2 who is cutting around and in back of #1.

Plays should be executed on call by the man without the ball. The play should be called by number or letter rather than by word. Plays *A* and *B* may be used with #2 having the ball. *B* then becomes a switch play as #1 should move into the place vacated by #2.

A should rarely be used when near opponent's goal line because of danger of ball going over end line and the difficult angle of centering the ball. *B* is a good play to use around the penalty area line as it gives #2 a possible shot or an easy center. *C* is indicated when the ball is within a few yards of the goal line. These plays may be used by the inside and the center forward or by the inside and the wing. Practice without opposition and then against one back.

39. Three Man Combination Play Drill

Play *D* is a pass back to the halfback by either #1 or #2. The halfback should dribble the ball while 1 and 2 continue to run forward until the halfback has drawn an opponent. The halfback may pass to either 1 or 2, whichever calls for play *A*.

Play *B* would be a through pass to 2 only. 1 should move toward the center of the field to draw his marker out of the way. (*See following page for illustration.*)

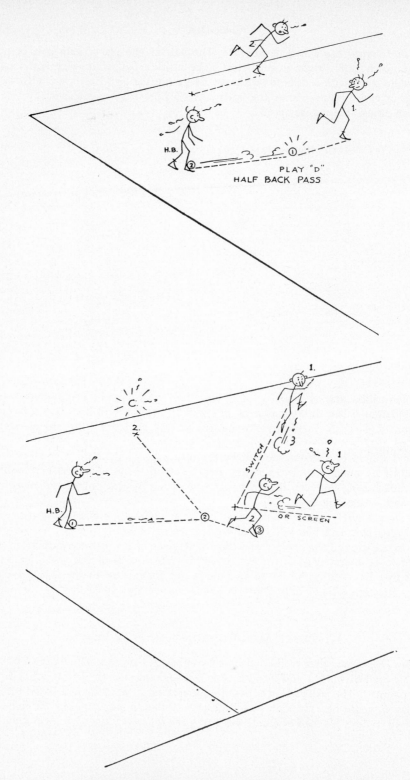

PLAY "D"
HALF BACK PASS

THREE-MAN COMBINATION PLAY DRILL

Play *C* may be used on call by #2, in which case #1 has the choice of moving toward the center of the field and screening or obstructing for 2, or of switching to #2's position.

A *B* play called by either #1 or by the center forward as a *C* play is completed will often place a man in a scoring position.

Practice until the players have developed the habit of advancing and calling the plays correctly before adding opposition.

In adding opposition, use one back, then two, and then three. When two or three backs are used, most of the likely game situations are covered. Practice all forwards and all backs and combinations thereof to make sure that all understand the signals.

40. Position Drill

The forward line starts from the center of the field and attacks against two full-backs and the goalkeeper. Concentrate on players holding proper position and calling combination plays.

41. Half-Field Scrimmage Drill

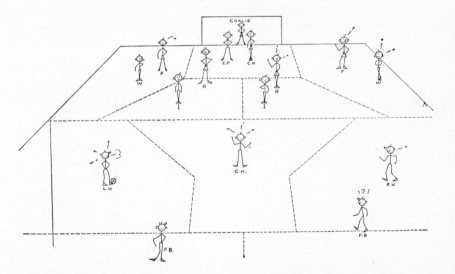

Spot the attacking team in the position that you want them to occupy when the ball is near the opponent's goal. Point out to them the territory in which they should cover the ball. (The assigned areas as illustrated above should be changed to meet the type of attack being used.) Use five defensive players and a goalkeeper to protect the goal. Have one of the halfbacks put the ball in play by a pass to a forward. When the ball is cleared the backs pass it up to the forwards. The forwards should keep continually moving in their territory in order to be in position to receive a pass from the backs. The center half should be encouraged to dribble in and shoot or to dribble in, draw a back and then pass to the unmarked forward.

42. Position Play Drill

Have the forwards attack with the ball on the wing and the backs defending according to zone or man-for-man defense. Use substitute forwards until backs are well trained in their duties, then use substitute offensive halfbacks to make the attack stronger.

43. Marking Drill

Any number of forwards on the field each with a back assigned to mark them. The forwards dodge, pivot, and use change of pace to get away from their marker. The coach starts and stops the drill by blowing a whistle. The back has his man marked if he can touch his forward each time the second whistle blows.

44. Varied Soccer

Eight-a-side is played with four forwards, three backs, and a goalkeeper. Areas that are too small for a regular playing field can be used for this game. It will afford opportunity for players, who might otherwise be standing on the sidelines, to develop individual skills and stamina. The off-side rule may be used.

Six-a-side may be used outside but is a better game for the gymnasium. When used indoors, use a volleyball, small goals (ice-hockey size), abolish the off-side rule, and use no goalkeeper. In this game it is a penalty to stop in front of the goal unless closely guarding an opponent.

APPENDIX II

Games to Make Practice Fun

1. TARGET SHOOTING (ACCURACY OF AIM)

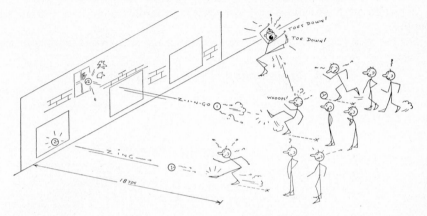

Use the instep kick or any of its variations to hit a target drawn on a wall or bounding board. Score one for a ball that hits the line. Score two points for a ball hitting entirely within the target. Use no more than three players to a target. Winner is the first one to score ten points.

2. PLACEMENT KICKING (ACCURACY OF AIM AND POWER)

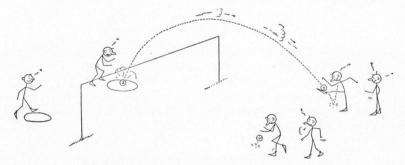

The object is to drop the ball into the circle by a volley kick over the goal from behind the restraining line. Each player bounces the ball for himself. Players take turns in kicking and fielding the ball. Score as for target shooting.

3. KICK FOR DISTANCE (FIRST TIME POWER KICKING)

Team A starts game by kicking to Team B. Team B returns the kick, and the game continues. The object is to force the opponents back toward their goal line. That team wins which first kicks the ball over the opponents' goal line. The weak foot of each player is indicated by rolling down the sock or by some other means.

Rules—If the ball is trapped, it must be kicked by the player's weak foot.

If the ball is kicked without trapping, it may be kicked with either foot.

The player who first touches the ball must kick it.

A ball kicked over the side line is put in play where it went out, with a strong-foot placement kick.

Penalties.—For intentional use of hands, 10 yards from where ball is finally stopped.

For toe kick, 15 yards from where kick was made and kick is taken over again.

4. ELIMINATION (VOLLEY KICKING)

Six players scattered around the field about 20 yards apart. The player in whose direction the ball goes must volley it. If it hits the ground three times or he misses his kick, he is eliminated from the game.

5. WALL BALL (BALL CONTROL)

The game may be played against a wall, building, or bounding-board. It is played like one-wall handball with two players on each team. The rules are the same as for handball with the following exceptions: (1) the ball is kicked, (2) the ball is put in play (served) by means of a half-volley kick, (3) the ball may bounce three times before being returned against the wall provided it is played between each bounce by the head, body or feet.

6. KICKING DUEL (GOALKEEPER SKILLS)

Two goalkeepers attempt to force each other back by using drop-kicks. The kick is taken from the place where the ball is caught. A ball fumbled is penalized by the loss of ten yards. The player wins who first backs his opponent off the field. Repeat using the weak foot.

7. Soccer Tennis (Ball Control)

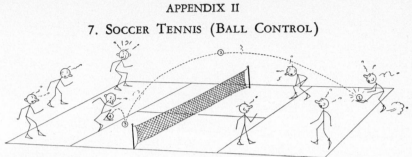

The game is played with four or five on each team. The rules are the same as for tennis except: (1) the service is taken with a half-volley kick, (2) the ball may not be headed over the net, (3) it may be played three times before being returned, but must go over on the third play, (4) it may bounce only once before being played.

8. Scramble (Over-head Kicking)

Scatter any number of players around the field. Count one point for each successful over-head kick. The first player to score five points is the winner. Any or all players may attempt to kick the ball at the same time. When at any time the ball stops bouncing it is out of play and is put back in play by any player kicking it into the air.

9. Circle Keep-away (Passing, Feinting, Trapping)

Players form in a circle and try to keep the ball away from "it" in the center. If "it" legally touches the ball, the last man to touch the ball becomes "it." "It" may go after the ball wherever it is played whether in or outside the circle. The game may be made more difficult by using the rule that the ball must be kicked without being trapped.

10. KEEP UP (LOB KICKING)

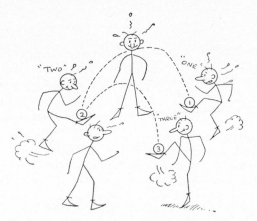

Players are formed in groups of five. They attempt to keep the ball in the air by using lob kicks. No player may kick the ball twice in succession. Count the number of successive lobs before the ball hits the ground. If the ball hits the ground, the count starts over again. The group having the most number of consecutive lobs is the winner.

11. DRIBBLING RELAY (DRIBBLING)

Half of each team lines up in front of half of the other team. At the command "go" the first player in each line dribbles in and out around the defensive players, and returns the ball to the next player who may then start his dribble. The defensive players may kick the ball as it passes in front of or in back of them provided they have one foot in place. The team finishing first is the winner and scores one point. For the second half of the race the dribblers and the defensive men change places. The game may be made more difficult for the dribblers by shortening the distances between the defensive men.

12. KEEP UP (HEADING)

Players compete in groups of two or three to see which group can make the most successive "heads." Rules are the same as for game 10.

13. HEADING TRAVEL (DIRECTIONAL HEADING)

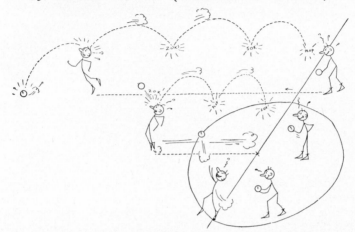

Players attempt to travel down the field by heading the ball forward successively. The player traveling farthest from the starting line to the place where he last headed the ball is the winner. To start his attempt the player throws the ball as far forward as he wishes.

14. HEADS UP (PLACEMENT HEADING)

A ball is tossed up between two players who attempt to so head it that they may get it under control. The one so doing, scores one point for his team. A foul scores one point for the opponents. A ball is considered under control when a player has his foot on it.

15. ODD MAN (HEADING)

A, the odd man, throws the ball to B and then attempts to recover the headed ball. (The ball is considered recovered if the foot is on it.) B has the choice of heading to C or to himself. If B or C succeed in recovering the ball, A is still the odd man and throws it to C. When the "odd man" recovers the ball, the player to whom it was thrown becomes the "odd man." This places the responsibility for a successful pass on the player doing the heading. The players will soon learn to feint and to judge where a ball is being headed, both of which are valuable assets.

16. TWO AGAINST TWO (ALL SKILLS)

Use Drill No. 28 and by counting one point for each successful pass keep a score. The first pair of players to score ten points is the winner.

17. SOCCER VOLLEY-BALL[1] (BALL CONTROL)

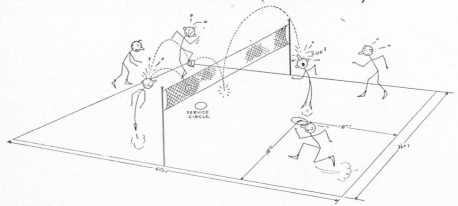

Three to five players on each team. Size of court—36' x 60'. Top of net—7' from ground.

[1] William Jeffrey, Vol. II, No. III, p. 8, *The Soccer Journal of the National Soccer Coaches Association of America.*

Each man on both sides takes his turn to serve with a header over the net to the opposing team. After service either feet or head are used. The ball may be played three times before returning it over the net to the opposition, with the allowance of one bounce between each play. Failure to return the ball at the end of three plays, or to allow the ball more than one bounce between plays, or playing the ball out of the opponent's court gives the point to the opposition. Fifteen points constitute a game. The game must be won by a margin of two points.

18. THREE ATTACK THREE (PASSING, SHOOTING, TACKLING)

Three players attack the goal, which is defended by the other team of three. The three attackers start from the penalty area line, while the three defenders must remain in the goal area until the attack starts.

Rules.—No player may use his hands on the ball. Any foul committed is an indirect free kick. Sides are changed when the defense kicks the ball out of the penalty area, or the attack kicks the ball over the goal line. If the attack scores a goal, they again attack. When the defense plays the ball over the end line, the attack kicks it in.

The winner may be determined by fixing the number of goals to terminate the game, or by setting a time limit.

Regulation goals need not be used, as smaller ones or substitutes will answer the purpose.

19. Mass Dribbling (Dribbling and Tackling)

Make a game out of Drill No. 30 by scoring one point for each ball successfully carried across the field, and alternating the dribblers with the tacklers.

20. Work Up (Dribbling, Obstructing, Shooting)

1 tries to dribble in and shoot a goal. He is aided by 2, who attempts to obstruct 3. 2 may receive and pass the ball but may not shoot. If the shot is missed, 3 takes 2's place, 2 moves up to 1, and 1 becomes 3. Provided 3 gets control of the ball, he changes place with the last one to play it. The goalkeeper remains constant. The player scoring the most goals is the winner.

21. Walking Scrimmage

This is a regular game played at slow speed which permits the coach time to correct the position play of both the defense and the offense.

Rules.—Regular rules plus the awarding of a free kick for opponent running. A walk is defined as having one foot on the ground. When both feet are off the ground it is a run. The kick may be either direct or indirect, whichever best suits the purpose of the coach.

22. Weak Foot Scrimmage

Regular scrimmage and rules are used with the addition of the penalty of a free kick if the ball is passed, kicked, or trapped with the strong foot. The strong foot of each player should be indicated by rolling the stocking down, tieing a handkerchief around it, or some other method.

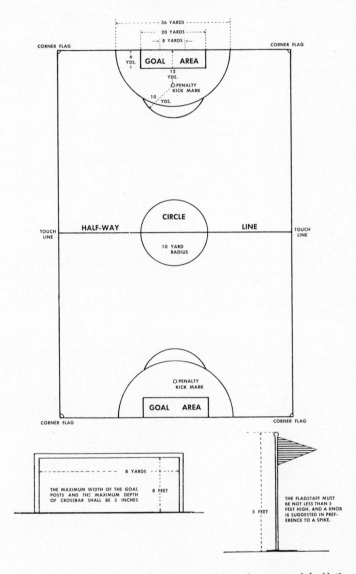

36 YARDS
20 YARDS
8 YARDS
CORNER FLAG   CORNER FLAG
6 YDS.
GOAL   AREA
12 YDS.
PENALTY KICK MARK
10 YDS.
CIRCLE
TOUCH LINE   HALF-WAY   CIRCLE   LINE   TOUCH LINE
10 YARD RADIUS
PENALTY KICK MARK
GOAL   AREA
CORNER FLAG   CORNER FLAG

8 YARDS
THE MAXIMUM WIDTH OF THE GOAL POSTS AND THE MAXIMUM DEPTH OF CROSSBAR SHALL BE 5 INCHES   8 FEET

5 FEET
THE FLAGSTAFF MUST BE NOT LESS THAN 5 FEET HIGH, AND A KNOB IS SUGGESTED IN PREFERENCE TO A SPIKE.

Reproduced through courtesy of the National Collegiate Athletic Association, copyright 1960

Intercollegiate Marking of Field, 1961

Index

A

Amateur Athletic Union, 5
Angle of Possible Shot, 61, 69
Anticipation, 58, 74
Attack
  Long Passing, 118
  Short Passing, 120

B

Back-Heel Pivot, 55
Ball Control, 40
Balls, 11, 12
  Care of, 13
Bouncing by goalkeeper, 64
Bounding Ball Traps, 36, 37
Bounding Boards, 9, 10, 18

C

Catching by goalkeeper, 58, 59, 60
Center Forward
  Position Play, 78
  Skills, 78
  Suggestions, 79
Center Halfback
  Position Play, 72, 73
  Skills, 73
  Suggestions, 73, 74, 75
Charging
  Definition of, 44
  Rule on, 47
  Technique of, 47
Chest Trap, 37, 38, 54
Corner flags, 9
Corner Kick
  Defense, 97, 98
  Offense, 98, 99, 100
  When allowed, 97

D

Defensive Center Forward Formation, 126
Deflection Trap, 35, 36
Diagrams, Legend for, 80
Dimensions of fields, 167
Diving, 61
Dodging
  Goalkeeper, 64
  With Ball, 51, 52
Dribbling
  Deceptive, 52, 53
  Inside of Foot, 40
  Outside of Foot, 40, 41
  Proper use of, 39
Drills
  Backs Against Forwards, 152
  Blind Shooting, 148
  Calling for the Ball, 153
  Center and Shoot, 143
  Corner Kick, 142
  Cross, Center, and Shoot, 144
  Deflection Trap, 149
  Deflection and Dodge, 150
  First-Time Kicks, 142
  First-Time Volley, 145
  Five Man Quick-Breaking, 154
  Free Goal Shooting, 142
  Half Field Scrimmage, 157
  Head and Dodge, 150
  Head for Goal, 150
  Heel or Sole Pass, 149
  Lob and Dodge, 147
  Lob and Evade, 147
  Long Kick, 142
  Marking, 158
  Mass Tackling, 152
  Obstructing, 152
  Over-Head Kick and Dodge, 145
  Over-Head Kicking (Long), 145
  Parallel Lines, 141
  Pass Scoring, 146
  Playing the Ball, 151
  Position, 157
  Position Play, 158
  Receive and Shoot, 141
  Stopping a Dribbler, 153
  Stopping Two Men, 153
  Three Man Combination Play, 155, 156, 157
  Three Man Quick-Breaking, 154
  Three on Two, 148
  Throw-In and Lob, 147
  Trap Scoring, 149
  Triangle Heading, 150
  Triangle Volley, 144
  Two Against Two, 151
  Two Men Combination Play, 155
  Two on One, 146
  Volley Kick, 144
Drop Ball, 100
Drop Kick, 25, 26
Duties of players, 67

E

Eight-Man Soccer, 158-167
Evasion Dodge, 51

F

Factors in Passing, 34
Federation Internationale de Football Association, 5
Feints, 50
Fly Ball Traps, 38, 39
Formations of Attack and Defense
  Defensive Center Forward, 126, 127
  Third Back, 122-125
  "W" with Roving Center Halfback, 120, 121, 122
Forward, Center
  Position Play, 78
  Skills, 78
  Suggestions, 79, 80
Forwards, Inside
  Position Play, 77
  Skills, 78
  Suggestions, 79, 83
Forwards, Outside
  Position Play, 75
  Skills, 76
  Suggestions, 79, 80
Free Kick
  Direct, 104, 105, 106
  Indirect, 101, 102, 103, 104
Fullbacks
  Position Play, 70, 71
  Suggestions, 73, 74, 75
Fundamentals, Method of presenting, 18, 19
Fundamentals Evaluated, 54

G

Games
  Circle Keep Away, 161
  Dribbling Relay, 162
  Elimination, 160
  Heading Travel, 163
  Heads Up, 163
  Keep Up (Heading), 163
  Keep Up (Kicking), 162
  Kick For Distance, 160
  Kicking Duel, 160
  Mass Dribbling, 166
  Odd Man, 164
  Placement Kicking, 159
  Scramble, 161
  Soccer Tennis, 161
  Soccer Volley-Ball, 164
  Target Shooting, 159
  Three Attack Three, 165
  Two Against Two, 164
  Walking Scrimmage, 166
  Wall Ball, 160
  Weak Foot Scrimmage, 166
  Work Up, 166
Glossary, 136, 137
Goal, Construction of
  Ideal construction, 7
  Movable, 8
  Suitable substitutes, 7, 8
Goalkeeper
  Anticipating, 58
  Bouncing, 64
  Catching, 58, 59, 60
  Diving, 61
  Dodging, 64
  Kicking, 65, 66
  Position Play, 69
  Punching, 62
  Selection of, 68
  Skills, 70
  Stance, 57
  Striking, 63
  Throwing, 65
  Tipping ball, 60
Goal Kick
  Goalkeeper, 66
  Opponents' kick, 94, 95
  Own kick, 95, 96
Goals nets, Methods of supporting, 8

H

Halfbacks, Wing
  Position play, 71
  Skills, 72
  Suggestions, 73, 74, 75
Half-Volley Kick, 25, 26
Harpastum, 3
Heading
  From Forward to Backward, 42
  From Forward to Forward, 41
  From Forward to Sideward, 42, 43
Heel pass, 32

I

Indoor Soccer, 158
Inside Forwards
  Position Play, 77
  Skills, 78
  Suggestions, 79, 80
Inside of Foot
  Dribble, 41
  Lob, 29, 30, 31
  Pass, 29
  Trap, 37
  Trap and Pivot, 56
Instep Kick
  Outside-of-the-Foot, 21, 22
  Pivot, 22, 23, 24
  Simple, 19, 20, 21
Intercollegiate Soccer Football Association of America, 5

K

Kick, Choosing proper, 27, 28
Kick-In Plays, 86-93
Kicking by Goalkeeper, 65, 66
Kick-Off Plays
  Defense against, 83, 84
  Offense, 81, 82, 83

L

Laws, Questions and Answers, 110, 114
Legend for Diagrams, 80
Long Passing Attack, 118, 119

M

Marking out fields, Methods of
  Dry lime, 7
  Wet lime, 7

N

Names of Players
  Eight-man team, 67
  Eleven-man team, 67
National Amateur Challenge Cup Competition, 5
National Challenge Cup Competition, 5
National Football Associations, 4, 5
National Soccer Coaches Association of America, 5

O

Obstructing, 48
Off-Side, 96, 97
One-Leg Tackle, 45, 46
Outside-of-Foot Instep Kick, 21, 22
  Dribble, 40, 41
  Pass, 31
Over-Head Kick
  Long, 26, 27
  Short, 33

P

Passing, Methods of
  Factors in, 34
  Heel, 32
  Inside of Foot (Push pass), 29
  Inside of Foot Lob, 29, 30, 31
  Outside of Foot (Flick or jab), 31
  Overhead, 33
  Sole of Foot, 32
Penalties, 101
Penalty Kick
  Defense, 107
  Kicker, 107
  Offense, 108
  When Allowed, 106
Pivot
  Back-Heel, 55
  Instep-Kick, 22, 23, 24

  Screen, 56
  Tackle, 46
  Trap and, 56
Position of Players, 67
Principles of Coaching, 129-135

R

Referee, suggestions for, 109
Relaxed Leg Trap, 37
Rolling Ball Traps, 35, 36
Running, 50

S

Sane Soccer for Elementary Schools, 126
Screen Pivot, 56
Selecting a team, 68
Shin guard, 11
Shoes, 10
Short Passing Attack, 120
Side of Foot Trap, 35
Side of Leg Trap, 39
Simple Instep Kick, 19, 20
Sole of Foot
  Pass, 32
  Tackle, 45, 46, 47
  Trap, 35, 36, 38
Stance of Goalkeeper, 57
Starting a Game, 81
Stockings, 11
Stomach Trap, 37, 38
Striking by goalkeeper, 63
Soccer, Forms of
  American, 5
  Derivation of name, 4
  English, 3, 4, 5
  Greek, 3
  Roman, 3
  Scope of, 4, 5
Switch Plays, 128

T

Tackling
  Definition of, 44
  One-Leg, 45, 46
  Pivot, 46
  Sole-of-the-Foot, 45, 46, 47
  Two-Leg, 44
Third Back Formation, 122, 123, 124
Thring, J. C., 4
Team Offense and Defense (Eleven-Man)
  Formations, 120-127
  Long Passing Attack, 118, 119
  Principles of, 118
  Short Passing Attack, 120
Throwing
  Goalkeeper, 65
  Regulation two-hand, 49
Throw-In or Kick-In Plays
  Defense against, 88, 90, 92, 93

Offense, 86, 87, 89, 91
Tipping ball, 60
Trapping
  Bounding-Ball
    Chest, 37, 38, 54
    Inside of Foot, 37, 56
    Relaxed Leg, 37
    Sole of Foot, 36
    Stomach, 37, 38
  Definition of, 34
  Fly Ball
    Side of Leg, 39
    Sole of Foot, 38
  Rolling Ball
    Deflection, 35, 36
    Side of Foot, 35
    Sole of Foot, 35

U

United States Soccer Football Association,
  5

V

Volley Kick, 24
  Half, 25, 26
  Jump, 25
  Knee, 24
  Scissors, 25
Varied Soccer, 158

W

"W" Formation with Roving Center Half-
  back, 120-121
Warm-up, Methods of
  Fundamentals, 16, 17
  Mass exercises, 15
Wing Forwards
  Skills, 76
  Position Play, 25
  Suggestions, 79, 83
Wing Halfbacks
  Position Play, 71
  Skills, 72
  Suggestions, 73, 74, 75

THE ARCO SPORTS LIBRARY

CHAMPIONSHIP WRESTLING
Clifford Keen, et al

A comprehensive manual for amateur wrestlers, coaches and instructors covering every stage of development from beginning to Olympic competition, with a special chapter on Greco-Roman wrestling. Photographs showing hundreds of holds illustrate the text.

Clothbound: $4.50; Paperbound: $3.95

GYMNASTICS AND TUMBLING
Hartley Price, et al

A complete course in the principles and methods of gymnastics and tumbling—equipment requirements and care, terminology, warm-up and conditioning exercises, safety methods and devices, apparatus, climbing and balancing, trampoline activities. Detailed explanation for executing each exercise are accompanied by photographs illustrating the progression of movements. **Paperbound: $4.95**

MODERN FENCING
Clovis Deladrier

The fundamentals, principles and finer points of the three weapons used in modern fencing—the foil, the epee and the sabre. Over 100 clear photographs illustrate chapters on preliminary phases, the parries, simple and compound attacks, the Riposte and Counter-Riposte, preparations for the attack, special exercises.

Paperbound: $3.95

SWIMMING AND DIVING
John Higgins et al

A thorough guide to the technique of swimming and diving. Includes basic swimming instruction for all strokes, material on competitive swimming, water polo and other games, competitive diving and life saving skills. Special appendix includes Olympic swimming and diving records. Fully illustrated. **Paperbound: $4.95**

SOCCER
Earle Waters, et al

Contains the history, principles and techniques of a universal game—equipment and safety suggestions, warm-up periods, individual fundamentals, the goal-keepers skills, analysis of individual positions, game situations, team offense and defense, principles of coaching. Generously illustrated. **Paperbound: $3.95**

SQUASH RACQUETS
Arthur M. Potter

Photos of strokes and playing situations illustrate this exhaustive guide to singles and doubles squash. Covers squash etiquette, tactics, training, mechanics of the stroke and the service. Playing rules and a guide to scoring included. **Paperbound: $3.95**

Available at all bookstores or directly from

ARCO PUBLISHING COMPANY, INC.,
219 Park Avenue South, New York, N.Y. 10003

ARCO SPORTS BOOKS

ARCHERY

Edmund Burke

Comprehensive illustrated course in all facets of archery from target, field and flight to the history of this ancient sport.
Paperbound: $1.45

ARCHERY HANDBOOK

Edmund Burke

Over 200 photos show step-by-step proper shooting techniques, target archery, hunting with bow and arrow, practice exercises, more.
Clothbound: $3.50

THE COMPLETE ARCHERY BOOK

Louis Hochman

America's top archers—Howard Hill, Joe Fries and Bob Markworth reveal techniques that make it possible for everyone to handle the bow and arrow with ease and accuracy. 262 illustrations.
Clothbound: $3.50

FIELD AND TARGET ARCHERY

Edmund Burke

285 show-how photographs illustrate archery technique, tricks, patterns and positions. Designed to help archers improve their style and scoring.
Clothbound: $4.00

ALL ABOUT FENCING

Bob Anderson

Over 400 unique stop-action sequence photographs explain and illustrate the fundamentals of foil fencing. Includes everything from direct attack to parry and riposte.
Clothbound: $4.50; Paperbound: $1.65

HOW TO TRAIN FOR TRACK AND FIELD

Peter Hildreth

Complete handbook for track and field athletes including sprinting, hurdling, middle- and long-distance running, jumping, vaulting and throwing, with the history and background of each event. Fully illustrated.
Paperbound: $1.45

HUNTING WITH BOW AND ARROW

George Laycock and Erwin Bauer

More than 100 action photographs illustrate how to use a bow and arrow to hunt game of all sizes—everything from squirrels to elephants. Separate chapters devoted to bow fishing, hunting birds and archery games.
Clothbound: $3.50

THE MASTER DIVER AND UNDERWATER SPORTSMAN

Captain T.A. Hampton

Completely new and revised edition of the standard work on diving—breathing apparatus, air supply, diving suits, deep and coastal diving, underwater fishing, tides, currents, positions at sea, underwater photography, more. 91 drawings, 33 photographs.
Clothbound: $5.95

PLAY BETTER GOLF

John Jacobs

One of the game's top professionals explains the fundamentals and fine points of the game with the aid of over 65 action photographs.
Clothbound: $4.50; Paperbound: $1.45

PLAY BETTER TENNIS

Tony Mottram

Top professionals John Newcombe, Charlie Pasarell and Virginia Wade blueprint winning tennis technique—with 370 unique sequence photographs that provide a moving picture of the strokes when the pages of the book are flipped backward and forward.
Clothbound: $4.50. Paperbound: $1.65

SKI RACING—ADVICE BY THE EXPERTS

Curtis W. Casewit

All the suspense and color of international ski racing—ski technique, ski history, ski medicine—told from the point of view of established champions—Jean Claude Killy, Karl Schranz, Stein Erikson and scores more. 233 illustrations, large oversize format.
Paperbound: $1.95

Available at all bookstores or directly from

ARCO PUBLISHING COMPANY, INC.,

219 Park Avenue South, New York, N.Y. 10003